THE LAST
IMPRESARIO

PETER KLEIN

THE LAST IMPRESARIO

A THEATRICAL JOURNEY FROM TRANSYLVANIA TO TOSCANA

THE LAST IMPRESARIO

A THEATRICAL JOURNEY FROM TRANSYLVANIA TO TOSCANA

PETER KLEIN
PHYLLIS URMAN-KLEIN, PHD
2023

Copyrighted Material

The Last Impresario: A Theatrical Journey from Transylvania to Toscana

Copyright © 2023 by Dante Editore. All Rights Reserved.

No part of this publication may be reproduced, stored in a retrieval system or transmitted, in any form or by any means—electronic, mechanical, photocopying, recording or otherwise—without prior written permission from the publisher, except for the inclusion of brief quotations in a review.

For information about this title or to order other books and/or electronic media, contact the publisher:

Dante Editore
Via di Valle 12
Fiesole, Italy
peterkleinyc.com
peterklein77@aol.com

ISBNs:
979-8-9851972-0-4 (Hardcover with jacket)
979-8-9851972-1-1 (eBook)

Printed in the United States of America

Cover and Interior design: 1106 Design

Dedication

To my wife, Phyllis, whose commitment and talent gave my memoir wings, our daughters, Nadia and Alexis, our inspiration and to our grandchildren, Leo, Elodie, and Stella—our stars and legacy.

Around

the World

Contents

Acknowledgments		xiii
Prologue: *A Soaring Moment*		xvii
1	*Transylvania Revisited*	1
2	*Growing Up in Timişoara*	11
3	*Israel*	25
4	*There Would Be Music*	35
5	*The New World Awaits*	41
6	*A Life-Altering Encounter*	51
7	*The Birth of Living Arts*	63
8	*So Much Depends Upon . . .*	71
9	*A Segovia Reprise*	83
10	*The Spoleto Years*	93
11	*Cross-Cultural Challenges:* Swan Lake *to* A Chorus Line	111
12	*The Mafia Reigns*	131
13	*Liza*	139
14	**Tamara,** *A Playful Scherzo*	145

15	*Porgy and Me*	153
16	*Black and White*	165
17	*Building Bridges*	177
18	*Harmony in Israel*	189
19	*Reflections*	193
Notes		209
Bibliography		215
Index		217
About the Authors		227

Acknowledgments

Over the five-year saga from inception to completion, we have spoken to many who were crucial in completing this memoir, which has become my story but which Phyllis has contextualized, revealing the unique historical moment embedded in my career. Foremost, we want to thank Leslie Kendall Dye, our editor, whose thorough and talented writing enlivened and deepened our narrative.

From the initial contact at the Leonard Bernstein office raising the question of sponsorship for touring *West Side Story* in the early years to their suggestion that I contact Libby Smigel, head of the dance department at the Library of Congress, each conversation expanded our thinking about the American "arts" project. Libby's enthusiasm and encouragement fueled our curiosity to learn more and strengthen the intellectual rigor of our thinking.

When I happened upon a trailer of *Taking Venice*, by Amei Wallach, I was even more convinced that the '70s in Italy was a significant moment. Amei's insight and concurrence was much appreciated in understanding the pivotal moment of Rauschenberg's winning The Golden Lion.

Julia Foulkes, who curated the Jerome Robbins exhibit at Lincoln Center Library and David Vaughn, Merce Cunningham's manager, further

Prologue
A Soaring Moment

"We know what we are, but know not what we may be."
—WILLIAM SHAKESPEARE

ITALY, 1977

Hardly a breeze ruffled the palms and pink azaleas of Nervi. This Italian village is a garden sanctuary. Its wide, shaded paths are bordered by ancient trees; the park is awash with 100 varieties of roses, tended by expert Genovese gardeners. Footpaths wind to the harbor, where the waves crash on the rocks, and farther out, the sea is tranquil. Here, a summer day watching the waves on the sun-drenched beach creates an exquisite sense of peace.

Yet on this day, I looked up at Nervi's azure sky with panic. I was 31 and at the threshold of my new career. I watched the plane circling the airport with disbelief. I had chartered this flight from Bucharest myself—on the plane were 80 members of the American Ballet Theatre, who had just completed a tour in Romania—a gift from the U.S. State Department after a devastating earthquake. Here, the American Ballet Theater would join Baryshnikov, who had become a principal with ABT shortly after his defection from the Soviet Union, three years earlier. He had opted out of the Romanian leg of the journey, unwilling to return to the other side of the Iron Curtain, however briefly.[1]

I struggled to quell a rising tide of panic as the Tarom Romanian Airlines plane circled the Genoa airport for an hour because the local airport authorities refused to let their flight land. I was stuck inside the airport, trying desperately to reason with the Italian officials.

"*La prima è domani!*" I told them. "*L'aereo deve per forza atterrare!*" "The first performance is tomorrow! The plane must land!"

They gesticulated dismissively in the classic Italian style. "*Non è possibile. Mancano i documenti.*" "Impossible. Documents are missing."

They seemed to think this was a game. How could I make them realize it was dead serious? My first big break was a hair's breadth from disaster because of a bureaucratic glitch. And my career wasn't the only thing at stake: I had arranged for ABT to perform with Mikhail Baryshnikov for three nights at the prestigious Nervi Festival, which would be a historic first in the world of dance. But it wouldn't happen if these men refused to let the plane land.

It had all started in spring 1977 with a call from Mario Porcile (1921–2013), artistic director of the prestigious Nervi International Festival of Dance. It is held in July in a magnificent garden in the seaside town of Nervi, east of Genoa. Founded in the 1960s, the festival has long attracted glitterati and politicos from the Milan area who summer in the surrounding seaside resorts of Portofino, Santa Margherita, and Rapallo on the Italian Riviera, as well as the hilltop villages that dot the area and provide unsurpassed views of the sea.

Mario was a visionary who was fascinated by contemporary dance, which was considered quite daring at the time. Now he wanted me to find a world-renowned dancer for Nervi.

Prologue

I sought advice from Sheldon "Shelly" Gold of International Creative Management (ICM), with whom I worked at Sol Hurok's office. Shelly happened to be the agent for Baryshnikov.

As luck would have it, Baryshnikov was available. He was scheduled to tour with ABT in Western Europe. Fernando Bujones, Gelsey Kirkland, and a corps of eighty other ABT dancers had to be transported from Romania, with only a thirty-six-hour window until curtain. I chartered a Romanian plane at a competitive price, confident that it would be approved by the Italians. Although approval had not been granted, I naively had little concern.[2]

The plane departed July 6, 1977, still without a landing permit. I assumed landing would be easy to negotiate once the aircraft appeared on the horizon. How could they keep such an important group up in the air? It didn't seem, *per amor del' cielo,* very Italian! At the time, I was just beginning to understand the Italians, generally easygoing but, in this case, making it difficult because I hadn't hired an Italian charter.

The calm scene in the Nervi gardens was a stark contrast to the palpable tension around me, where airport authorities were gesticulating wildly and speaking in rapid-fire Italian, a language I was still struggling to master. It was embarrassing enough to have my girlfriend, Phyllis, standing a few feet away, watching the fiasco unfold, but making the situation even more unbearable was the fact that Baryshnikov himself was at my side. He was the last person I wanted to expose to this chaos. He had arrived from New York the night before. He was as dumbfounded as I was about the stalemate. Who would leave a plane full of human beings circling an airport this long just to quarrel over paperwork?

By this time, Alessandro Levrero, director of the Genoa Opera, had arrived to intercede for us and tried to emphasize to the airport officials that allowing the dancers to land was critical not only for the performance but for Italy's relationship with the USA.

"*Per favore, solo questa volta!*" he begged.

"*No,*" came the answer—nothing would budge them.

THE LAST IMPRESARIO

We had already contacted the American consulate, but there was little they could do. In desperation, we called the mayor of Genoa, hoping he could *risolvere il problema*. He finally appeared, flanked by police escorts. It was a grand entrance, indeed. I couldn't help noticing how displeased he looked. (I later learned that our frantic phone call had dragged him out of bed in the middle of a dalliance with his mistress.)

I was beginning to sweat bullets. What would happen if the plane ran out of fuel? Would air traffic control override the officials and give them permission to land for safety? Perhaps they would have made an exception for a soccer team, but, clearly, ballet mattered less here. I thought about all the anxious dancers stranded in the air with no explanation for the delay in landing.

It's unusual for me to freeze under pressure, but I was losing confidence. Fifteen years of living under communism had taught me that bureaucracies could disregard logic and red tape could control people completely. Why hadn't I foreseen this crisis? Booking the Romanian charter had seemed like a good idea at the time, but I had been hopelessly naïve to think I could overcome air traffic regulations just because I had a plane full of ABT dancers. I had jeopardized my first major career opportunity by trying to save a few thousand dollars.

The plane continued to circle the airport. Was there no one who could intervene?

At last, the Romanian pilot radioed the control tower. "We are running out of fuel," he said.

"*Sei securo?*"

"*Si!* We are running out of fuel!"

"*Allora, procedete ad atterrare!*" commanded the control tower. "All right, prepare to land!"

To our immense relief, the plane touched down a few minutes later. Our two buses pulled up to the tarmac, and the dancers walked lithely down the steps. We welcomed them with flowers and applause, then we whisked everyone to the hotel with no passport control. It seemed only gravity was forceful enough to overcome Italian red tape. *Viva Italia!*

Prologue

With this debacle behind me, I could now turn my attention back to other aspects of the tour, which was only my second with performing arts in Europe. The whole experience was fascinating and almost otherworldly, especially witnessing the exchanges of Florence Pettan (1930-2007), the ballet mistress, and the dancers. Little did I know how powerful her role was in the lives of the corp de ballet, let alone how significant it was for each dancer to have been selected for this tour.

Opening Night

Unexpected patches of clouds smeared the evening sky, creating an uneven glow and the dreaded possibility of rain—a rare phenomenon in early July—as festival-goers began to arrive. Backstage, the dancers were warming up and stretching as the *signore* made their way to their seats, splendidly arrayed in formal gowns, silk shawls, brocaded shoes, and Bulgari-quality estate jewelry that tended toward long strands of pearls and colorful brooches. I thought how much this contrasted with the simple country life of Liguria and realized that, in Italy, as in other European countries in 1977, mostly aristocracy and haute bourgeoisie attended this elite festival along with the intelligentsia. Performances on the level of ABT's were not easily accessible to the masses.

I was inundated with introductions to theater critics and the well connected, all of whom seemed excited about the evening ahead. It was difficult to determine who was important for me to meet, let alone remember who they were. At this point I only had a rudimentary knowledge of Italian. I recall looking at some of the business cards I'd collected when I returned to my room that night and having no memory of the people who had given them to me.

The program opened with *The Kingdom of the Shades*, the classic scene from *La Bayadère* by Marius Petipa, choreographed by Makarova. This was especially meaningful to me because it was the first ballet I saw at the Metropolitan Opera House, in 1969. The Italians were very receptive to this classic repertoire but curious about Twyla Tharp's *Push Comes to Shove*, which utilized unusual, contemporary choreography within a ballet company. (There were few, if any, contemporary dance companies in Italy at the time)[2.] By contrast, they were eagerly anticipating Baryshnikov, who had already earned international acclaim. A hush fell over the audience when he began to dance. Toward the middle of *Push Comes to Shove*, we heard a clap of thunder, and it started to rain, but Misha wove it brilliantly, making spontaneous, playful movements to the rhythm of the rain and pulling his T-shirt over his head in the middle of the piece. At that moment, the curtain closed, and everyone ran for shelter.

Fifteen minutes later, the rain stopped, and stagehands frantically swept the linoleum so that it would be in perfect condition for continuing. *Push Comes to Shove* continued with Misha in a mime position, with both arms up in the air. I exhaled with relief. The audience was delighted with Misha's humor and this surprising repertoire. It was fresh and exciting in contrast to the predictable, somewhat staid classical ballet they had known. The air felt charged with excitement, and, to my delight, the crowd erupted in enthusiastic applause at the end of the performance, while the dancers were showered with more flowers than one could count.

When the theater finally emptied, Alessandro Levrero, Mario Porcile, Florence Pettan, and I walked with a group of arts patrons down to the port in the idyllic seaside fishing village of Camogli. In true Italian style, the restaurateurs gladly postponed their closing for us, welcoming us with cries of, "*Venite! Mangiate!*" I particularly enjoyed the *cioppino*, the *acciughe in olio*, and the *mozzarella al forno*, which evoked the saltiness of the sea. We stayed late into the night, finally heading back to the villa in the early-morning hours, where I tumbled into bed and awoke around noon. I hurried out for a cappuccino and a newspaper and was relieved to see that the critics had given us outstanding reviews. I did not yet understand that, once the Italians put their faith in you, they often develop unrealistic expectations, somewhat idealizing what an American event can be.

Prologue

As I entered the dining room, I overheard Florence Pettan commenting to the dancers.

"Perfect."

"You were off a bit with the music . . ."

"You certainly enjoyed your Italian dinner last night . . ." Florence remarked sarcastically. Over a late breakfast, Florence discussed the injuries sustained in the previous night's performance and who would have to be replaced. I was astounded at the number of sprained ankles and torn ligaments incapacitating dancers, partly due to the rain and the slippery stage. I hoped we wouldn't have to draw upon understudies too much; I was only newly aware of the treacherous life of a ballerina. I remember watching Gelsey and the other dancers stretch and warm up, thinking they looked like they were torturing themselves. I was struck by what a study in contradiction they were: physically powerful but emotionally vulnerable, even fragile.

Since at open-air theaters there were no matinees, the dancers didn't go to the theater until about 7:30 p.m. for a 9:30 curtain. I remember the lead dancers lounging on the terrace in the late afternoon, their hair pulled back, wearing loose tops and long skirts. Florence wore a piano shawl and a simple but elegant long chiffon skirt. The scene reminded me of a Renoir painting. Sitting on the terrace of our stately hotel overlooking a manicured garden helped me relax before the evening's inevitable drama backstage, where one poorly fitted toe shoe could trigger a fit of hysterics, and the stress of trying to anticipate what I should do next. Despite Phyllis' reassuring presence and all the activity around us, I still felt lonely and uncertain about what was expected of me as a neophyte impresario.

The corps de ballet was pleased with its accommodations and seemed to bear no grudge about the landing delay, but I hadn't developed a relationship with the ballet administrators yet, so I wasn't sure what impact the airport fiasco would have on them. Nor was I sure how the Italians felt about my decision not to charter an Italian plane. Would they be reluctant to work with me again? Had I closed the door to future business? At this point in my fledgling career, it was all uncharted territory.

After a triumphant second night's performance, Alessandro and his wife invited Phyllis and me to their apartment for dinner. Being welcomed into the opera director's home for a private dinner was unexpected and flattering. Although he was in his forties and dressed stylishly in a suit and tie, he rode a motorcycle, and I sensed a bit of a bohemian, artistic side to him. He was fascinated by our New York lifestyle and asked whether we visited Harlem and where to find "hot" jazz. He was particularly inquisitive about how Black people were treated in America. I wasn't comfortable sharing my views on the extent of the racism I'd observed in the United States, but I promised to take him to Harlem the next time he visited New York. I did not yet grasp his eagerness for an entrée into New York life from a fellow European, someone he and his wife saw as similar to themselves.

I, in turn, was fascinated with their lifestyle. I wanted to know how they lived, what they ate, their views of Americans. Most of all, I hoped this dinner would provide an opportunity to get Alessandro's reaction to what had happened at the airport and to find out more about how funding for the arts was structured here. I didn't yet understand the formidable role politics played in the arts, how fast the sands could shift with a changing political landscape, or how readily the right connections could adjust the rules. I was, however, beginning to observe how the Italians did business.

The stakes were high, so I was wary of overstepping my bounds or offending the wrong people. But with no mentor in Italian culture and only a modest grasp of the language, finding my way was not easy. I wanted to plant a seed for bringing another dance performance to the festival the following year, but I wasn't sure how to open the discussion. What could I ask? What was taboo? I didn't even know if I had competitors in New York. I wasn't sure who made the final decisions in relation to budget and groups. I didn't even know whether positions like Alessandro's were

Prologue

temporary or permanent. This success at Nervi was a golden opportunity but also a delicate one.

After the second of the three performances, too full of emotions and possibilities to sleep, I returned on my own to Camogli. I needed time to reflect. The festival at Nervi was magical. The success of ABT and Baryshnikov, despite all the tension that preceded their performance, seemed like a dream. After immersing myself in ballet over these three days both backstage and front, I was enchanted with the discipline and mastery of the dancers. Ideas were swirling around in my head. I had worked backstage at the Metropolitan Opera in NY but in a more administrative role. I was intoxicated with possibilities now that a seed had been planted. Were there other American companies that could create this kind of excitement? What would be my next steps? As I lingered at Camogli alone, my mind wandered. I reflected on my life.

Gazing at the vista before me, I was struck by how far I had come. How had a Jewish Hungarian boy from Romania traveled to the United States with no money or obvious prospects, and wound up standing on a beautiful Italian coastline, an ambassador of the finest ballet company the United States had yet produced.

1

Transylvania Revisited

How did I find myself attempting to land a plane full of professional ballet dancers in Italy without a permit? Let me start at the beginning.

I grew up in Timișoara, a picturesque city in Transylvania, Romania. Although my family never discussed World War II, my Jewish roots and the horrors perpetrated by Romanian heads of state and Nazi sympathizers laid the foundation of my journey.

Jews have lived in southwestern Transylvania's Banat region since at least the second century AD. In Timișoara, you'll find graves in the old Sephardic cemetery dating from the Turkish occupation of the 1600s, although the first written official acknowledgment of the Jewish community there came in 1716, with the Peace Treaty of Passarowitz. The treaty ended Turkish rule and allowed Jewish citizens to remain under Austrian rule, if they chose to do so.[1]

Timișoara's Jewish community flourished in the 1800s, after the Austro-Hungarian Empire instituted citizens' rights acts, and eventually grew to a population of almost 7,000. By the late nineteenth century, the city boasted half a dozen synagogues.[2]

When World War I ended, the map of Europe was redrawn, and the Austro-Hungarian Empire was dismantled. Consequently, Transylvania became a part of Romania in 1920. In the decade that followed, the region's Jewish population thrived, assimilating into the community, attaining high-ranking government positions, and making inroads into elite sports like fencing. But as Jews became more prominent, an undercurrent of anti-Semitism swelled, gaining momentum during the mid-1930s.

In 1940, both Hungary and Romania allied with the Nazis. In Hungary, no Jews were spared the aim of the "Final Solution." They were to be systematically sent to the gas chambers.[3] Romania was hardly less perilous, particularly for Jews living in the east, who were often wrongly suspected of having links to Soviet Communism. Hungarian Jews in Transylvania were also associated negatively with Hungarian rule.[4]

In 1941, Romania's fascist dictator Marshal Ion Antonescu ordered the slaughter of Romanian Jews in Bessarabia and North Bukovina, which the USSR had recently annexed from Romania, on the pretense of quelling an uprising.[5] The Nazi Einsatzgruppe D was only too happy to oblige and, with cooperation from some of the locals, murdered between 100,000 and 120,000 people. Similar massacres occurred in Western Ukraine at the hands of the Romanian army, with some of the bloodiest in the city of Odessa.[6]

Survivors of the Bessarabia and North Bukovina massacres were rounded up along with Jews from South Bukovina and Romania's Dorohoi regions and forced into the ghettos and death camps of Transnistria in West Ukraine. The consequences were tragic: 120,000 people were killed or died from hypothermia, starvation, and disease.[7] All told, as many as 400,000 Jews were murdered in Romanian-controlled areas during Antonescu's dictatorship.

As a child, I never heard about these horrors. The stories my parents told emphasized their pride in their history. Still, though they occurred several hundred miles away, these tragedies undoubtedly had an impact on my family.

Transylvania Revisited

Anti-Semitic attitudes were pervasive in Timişoara. In 1936, the Romanian Iron Guard attacked a Jewish theater, exploding a bomb. Two Jews in the audience were killed, and many were wounded. In 1940, the government imposed economic restrictions on Jews and started confiscating Jewish property. Despite this less-than-welcoming environment, the town's Jewish population—which numbered 10,950 in 1941—increased to 11,788 in 1942, because many Jews from the surrounding area sought asylum in my hometown, where the local community provided relative protection.

My paternal grandfather, Eugene Klein, was an officer in the Austrian-Hungarian Army, decorated in WWI. My great-grandmother on my mother's side had been a baroness but lost her title when she married a commoner. I didn't know this piece of family history until 2005, when my uncle Gyuri, who had come to New York to celebrate my mother's eighty-fifth birthday, presented me with a napkin bearing a crest of a crown.

"How long have you had this?" I asked, incredulous. "Mom, did you know about it?"

She shrugged her shoulders and smiled.

My parents had always told us that we were "special," not like everyone else in our community, but I had assumed they meant that we were Jewish and Hungarian, nothing more. Despite the anti-Jewish sentiment and the ever-present ghosts of WWII, we were raised with more emphasis on our Hungarian heritage than on our Jewish one, although given those conditions, perhaps that is not so surprising.

My mother's stepfather, Leopold Wohlstein, married my grandmother shortly after her first husband died at 31. He left my grandmother, Szilàgyi Piroska, with two small children, a functioning vineyard, several real estate holdings, and a successful ice business in Buzias, a small town known for its hot springs and popular as a destination for mud baths in the 1920s and '30s. *Naci*—as my brother, Gabriel, and I called her—was a practical woman, and she knew she couldn't manage so many responsibilities. She sold her holdings, remarried, and moved from

Buzias—where, in 1920, my mother, Ari Wiener, had been born—to Timișoara, which was considered the "big city," with its cultural offerings and streetcars.

My step-grandfather, Leo, was an exceptionally sweet, warm, and wonderful man. He had the distributorship for Meissen, Herend porcelain, and other international brands, which allowed my mother to enjoy a comfortable childhood. She attended a private Jewish high school in Timișoara, but it was Hungarian in tradition, with few Jewish rituals. My parents and the other assimilated Jews with whom they socialized very much identified as Jews, but they identified equally as Hungarians, in language, cuisine, and culture. I wonder now about the insularity of their social world—why was it exclusively Jewish? Was it from habit? Or caution? My parents never expressed an overt lack of trust in gentiles, but perhaps because the Romanian and Hungarian culture at large was so anti-Semitic, perhaps distrust, or at least caution, was inevitable. At any rate, my grandmother's—and, eventually, Ari's—signature dessert was Hungarian—a 16-layer "*dobosh torte*," with a caramelized sugar glaze, which requires red-hot knives to precut the sugar glaze!

By 1938, my mother, Ari, had blossomed into an eighteen-year-old beauty with an aristocratic lineage. She was dating George Klein, the son of a respected family in Timișoara's Jewish Hungarian community. A charming *bon vivant* with an eye for mischief, George was fun and carefree, and Ari gravitated toward his whimsical and impulsive nature. But when Ari met Andrew, George's older cousin, she was instantly taken with his humanity, warmth, and strength of character. Witty, athletic, and charming, Andrew was more grounded than his younger cousin George. He had left high school in 1929 at age 16 to support his parents after his father's business closed and had already established himself as a successful businessman, selling textiles imported from Western European countries. As much fun as she had adventuring with George, it was Andrew who truly won Ari's love. And so, with a bit of tact and sensitivity to George's bruised ego, Ari and Andrew began seeing each other.

Transylvania Revisited

On a warm, sunny afternoon in the spring of 1939, Andrew rolled up to Ari's home on Strada Trandafirilor in his flashy Chevrolet coupe convertible, grinning proudly. He had just purchased one of the first convertibles in Timișoara. In fact, he was among the first people in the city to own an automobile imported from America. The coupe was a trophy on wheels.

Keys jingling in hand, Andrew bounded up the steps of Ari's front porch, taking them two at a time.

"Come with me for a drive in the country, Ari!" he said excitedly. "It couldn't be a more perfect day!"

Ari knew the country roads that led to the hills outside of town were narrow, winding, and mostly unpaved, so she demurred. How many times had she heard of trucks or passenger cars suffering punctured tires from the sharp rocks scattered across the road?

But Andrew was persistent.

"I'll make you a deal," he said. "If I get you home in one piece, you must promise to marry me."

He did, and, so, on August 13, 1939, under the chuppah of the Neolog Synagogue in Timișoara, my parents, hopeful and very much in love, became husband and wife. Ari was beautifully dressed in a long, lace wedding gown. They observed the rituals of a Jewish wedding—exchanging rings, reciting blessings, breaking a glass—more out of respect for tradition than because of their own religious beliefs.

Less than a month later, while my parents were honeymooning in the Carpathian Mountains, Germany invaded Poland.

As Europe plunged into the nightmare of WWII, it seemed that Transylvania would remain relatively protected. But as the Nazis made their way East, the persecution of Eastern European Jews intensified, and what had been a vague fear of the Nazi presence in Romania became a terrifying reality. As the clouds of war gathered over Transylvania, the world Ari and Andrew knew began to crumble.

As a matter of relative luck, King Michael I, the ruling monarch, had a mistress, Magda Lupescu, a charming and beautiful woman, with a Jewish

5

background. It was rumored that she had convinced the king to stop the mass deportation of Romanian Jews in Transylvania to Nazi concentration camps, and instead to establish forced-labor camps. Communities that did not ingratiate themselves to the throne were refused this safeguard. The work-camp system was a brutal but less-lethal alternative to the concentration camps of Germany and Poland.[8]

In 1941, less than two years after my parents' wedding, my father was ordered to a camp in the countryside of Arad, to a battalion just north of the city allocated to the repair and upkeep of Timișoara's national service roads and rail lines. Jewish women were not forced to enlist in the camps, but fear of what might happen to them in their husbands' absence drove many into hiding in the Transylvanian countryside. Though my parents were seldom able to communicate while my father was in Arad, occasionally he managed to bribe the camp captain to allow him freedom to go home on weekends with the understanding that he would return by 8:00 a.m. Monday morning. These visits were few and far between. Even less frequent were his reunions with my mother, because, when he was able to get back, my father often found a note from my mother explaining that she had taken refuge in the countryside and hoped to see him the next time he came.

In August 1944, nine months before the fall of Berlin, the Soviets liberated Romania, putting an end to the labor camps and sending the humiliated and downtrodden Jewish men home to their families.

My parents lost no time starting a family. I was born on July 22, 1945, a healthy, ten-pound baby. My parents had just purchased a spacious three-bedroom home on Vladica Badescu Street, near Piata Lahovari, one of the first in Timișoara with central heating, modern bathrooms, and a quaint little garden. We had a nurse and a maid. My father returned to selling textiles, and again his business flourished. Though the havoc wreaked by war reverberated through most of Europe, Timișoara enjoyed two or three blissful years essentially untouched after its liberation by the Russian army. My parents were able to pick up where they had left off, leading a comfortable upper-class existence.

But the innocence of that life ended abruptly in 1948, when the Communists took over. The Commies decreed that people's shops, businesses, and personal property no longer belonged to them; they were being "nationalized" (a euphemism for "stolen"). Bank accounts and cash became worthless overnight because the currency was changed. Citizens were ordered to turn all their jewelry and valuables over to the government. A dear relative of ours served many years in prison for trying to hold onto a few of his own possessions. Middle and upper class families who had owned their homes for generations were unceremoniously kicked out to make room for those whom the Communists could trust—the proletarians. Tens of thousands were forced to relocate to tiny, old apartments that offered few, if any, modern comforts.

Our family was not unscathed. Shortly after my brother Gabriel's birth in March 1948, the beloved home that my father had bought for his growing family was nationalized, and we were forced to move into my grandparents' home, a small two-bedroom, one-bathroom apartment. Under a roof that comfortably housed two people, a crowd of six now converged: my paternal grandparents, Iren and Eugene; my mother and father, Gabriel and me. This would be the Timișoara of my youth. I was not yet three, but I have a vivid memory of sitting in bed when my parents presented me with a "new Romanian coin" as if this was something special. Their desperate attempts to frame the devastation that they were confronting were palpable at every turn. A remnant of a prior life: I had a crystal potty that I'd received from Leo, my stepgrandfather, who had sold fine crystal and china before Communism forever altered our lives.

Still, compared to much of the Jewish youth in Timișoara under Soviet occupation, Gabriel and I were lucky. The Communists shut down my father's textile wholesale business, but the state hired him as chief accountant for Electromotor, a Communist-managed company with about 500 employees that specialized in manufacturing and selling rotating electrical machines and generators. Having come from relative wealth, our parents were cultured, well-educated people. They—and all four of our grandparents—spoke multiple languages, were well read, and, though they had never traveled beyond the borders of the old Austro-Hungarian Empire, understood the world. Circumstance pushed our family together physically, but it had always been close emotionally, and by virtue of our living situation, the bond I forged with my parents and grandparents was indelible. The lessons they taught me have lasted my entire life.

From age three to eighteen, my family—my two grandparents, my parents, Gabriel, and I—lived in a cramped two-bedroom apartment, on the second floor of a patrician two-story building, with elaborate wrought-iron work on the stairs and balcony. The kitchen was a large, cold room with a gas stove that had only one burner. We had no hot water, so we heated water on the stove for baths. We did not have a freezer, only an icebox that we used whenever we could get chunks of ice. It lasted for a day or two, which meant that most food lasted only a few days. Milk was not pasteurized, so it had to be boiled. We did not have toilet paper in the bathroom, but we were happy to use the Romanian Communist party newspaper, *Scintea*. This was the *only* use we had for that paper!

Despite living in such close quarters and having lost most of our material possessions, my parents managed to maintain a warm, harmonious, and nurturing environment. In fact, since my father's career as a businessman had been aborted, Gabriel and I became his projects. At an early age, I understood that there was no room for disagreements or upset over what we had lost. I had to be stoic.

The Timișoara my parents had known prior to 1948 was a refined and charming little city with several tram lines, a symphony orchestra, an elegant, almost-grand 700-seat opera house, theaters that performed plays in four languages, and an abundance of local bakeries, boutiques, and businesses. It was a multicultural haven where Hungarians, Romanians, Germans, Serbo-Croats, and Jews coexisted in peace and harmony. My Timișoara was a city robbed of its riches by the Russians and saturated in anti-Semitism. In the 1950s, Russian soldiers were patrolling the streets. The first Russian words I ever heard were *"Davay tchass'ii!"* "Give me your wristwatch!"

From the beginning, we had three things against us, as did our parents and most affluent Hungarian Jews in Romania.

First, being Hungarians in Romania meant we symbolized values that ran counter to Communist ideals. Hungarians were traditionally more educated, civilized, and affluent than Romanians, having been part of the Austro-Hungarian Empire, while Romania belonged to the much-less-developed Ottoman Empire. This meant we were unlikely to buy the party line and, therefore, we were under suspicion.

Second, we were Jewish in a country that, although it professed to be Communist, was still heavily Catholic and tolerated Christianity as long as it wasn't openly discussed.

Third, we were part of the erstwhile upper class. That made us enemies of the Communists, who trusted only their fellow *uneducated* proletarians, many of whom couldn't even read or write.

I felt like an outsider in every way. My family tongue was different. At home, my parents and grandparents secretly deconstructed or negated the propaganda taught at school. We felt like marginalized citizens thrust into a repressive and increasingly constricted world. Adding to my sense of isolation, my mother became more and more volatile under the pressures of the circumstances and was often unreasonable, threatening to leave the house if we misbehaved. My father enlisted my brother and me to soothe her.

Fortunately, my father was a calming influence at home. Despite his economy with words, he was very nurturing and engaged. He had suffered oppression, travail, and hardship, but he managed to be an exceptional parent, teaching Gabriel and me everything he knew. When he was a child, my grandparents had hired a live-in German tutor for him and his older brother, Miklos. They learned not only the language but also the German literary canon. By the time he was 10, my father was fluent. He passed his love of foreign languages on to Gabriel and me and cultivated our appreciation for poetry, literature, and classical music. Every evening he read aloud from Goethe, Schiller, and his favorite 20th-century writer and poet, Erich Kästner, translating the original text into Hungarian. His parents, too, had a seemingly endless knowledge of Western culture, art, and music despite never having traveled, and they shared as much as they could with us.

Our books provided a window to another world although it seemed unreal. My father invented a game in which we mastered the capitals of each country. It was a way of keeping the hope alive that, someday, we would be able to leave our Communist purgatory, the only world we knew. Upon reflection, it's hard for me to believe that I didn't tire of this repetitive exercise, but I needed it. My internal world became a rich source of pleasure. This defense against the onslaught of the outer world was hard to give up—it was not only rewarding, but it was something I could control.

We were hardly the only ones who dreamed of life on the other side of the Iron Curtain. The only Romanians who could apply to emigrate were ethnic Germans, who could emigrate to Germany, and Jews, who could go to Israel or the West. But applying for emigration came at a price: instantly, you became a second-class citizen. *How could you reject wonderful, fabulous Communism, in which we all stand shoulder to shoulder?* You were blacklisted, relegated to the lowest-level jobs. The children weren't allowed to go to college. Still, everybody who was eligible applied to leave. We saw it not only as the best option but also as a statement of defiance: life in Romania was intolerable; the risk was worth taking.

In 1947, there were more than 13,600 Jews in Timișoara who had survived the war. By 1956, there were only about 6,700—most of them had emigrated to escape the depravations and oppression of Communist rule.[9] In 1949, my parents started petitioning the State for the right to emigrate. It would be many years before our dream of freedom would become a reality.

2

Growing Up in Timișoara

Despite external threats and uncertainty, life continued in my hometown. We tried to focus on small pleasures and family activities. Family time became a welcome refuge from the tense environment outside our home—and much more important than it would have been if we had felt like part of the community. Yet in spite of the prejudice we endured, we clung to our old values.

Deprivation was a way of life. I didn't ride in a car until I was fifteen, when I took a taxi to the train station in 1960—ironic, considering that my father had owned one of the first American convertibles in town back in 1938. There were almost no cars in Timișoara in those days. Bicycles were our primary means of transportation in the city; the other was the streetcar—or tramway. When I was about four and Gabiel was a year old, Dad built small seats to mount on his bike and proudly pedaled us around town. The year before, he gave me my first bike. Although times were tough—and I was one of the few kids to have a bike at such a young age—there was very little theft. Bike locks and chains were unheard of.

Cycling was one of my father's favorite hobbies, so it became important to me, too. Dad made sure all four of us had bicycles, for both sport and recreation. On Sundays, we would ride for hours, picnicking in the woods or by the locks on the Bega Canal. I loved watching the boats being guided through the powerful opening and closing gates. What technology! The Bega became one of our favorite spots for escaping the challenges of daily life, and we would sit with Uncle Leo, my step-grandfather, for hours, watching the water flow and pretending to fish while listening to his engaging stories, from the time I was five until I turned twelve.

Always passionate about athletics, my dad also taught us rowing, skiing, and tennis. He was slender, but muscular, well-proportioned, and athletic. He walked slowly and deliberately, but, on the tennis court, he was agile and precise.

I started playing tennis with my father regularly when I was about eight, and I continue playing to this day. He always served me a light breakfast before playing, even if I was ravenous. And after a workout, he believed in eating only fruit with a glass of milk. I played basketball on my high school team, but tennis was my real passion. In the spring of 1960, before I turned fifteen, I won second place in a fourteen to sixteen singles Banat regional tournament. I've spent more than half a century on tennis courts around the world and taken many, many lessons. Although I must admit that my level of playing does not reflect it, but I truly enjoy the game.

I admired my father most for his dignity. He often wore a suit or a jacket. He took a regular siesta on weekends and relished his rituals—no doubt to counter the instability of our lives. I can still see him taking his afternoon nap after a double espresso. He would settle into his favorite

Art Deco armchair, tuck his right hand halfway under his belt, and sail off for an hour or so. We all knew to be quiet while he slept.

There were brief moments when the horrors of WWII haunted me, but, as a child, it was hard to bring them into focus. My father was a man of few words. He rarely spoke of his time in the Arad camp. Knowing how Jews had been treated in the camps across Europe, I was hesitant to pry. But one morning when I was eight, as I sat on the edge of his bed, watching him dress for work, Dad said something I would never forget. As he tucked his shirt in and threaded his brown leather belt through the loops of his trousers, he looked in the mirror and paused. "Never thought I'd be grateful for a belt," he said, shaking his head.

He must have caught my puzzled look because he turned to me and, tightening the belt around his waist, said, "You know, Peter, they never let us wear these in Arad. The captains made us wear pants two sizes too big. Without a belt or a rope to hold them up, they would constantly fall down around our ankles while we were working in the rail yard or digging ditches along the road. There we'd be, stooping in the fields, breaking our backs, and slogging for hours, all for the camp guards' entertainment."

He stood with his hands on his hips, looking out the bedroom window. "From time to time, when the guards were bored, they would force us to mount their workhorses bareback and then spur them into a gallop, laughing and betting to see who could hang on while holding up his pants. I always pitied the men who didn't know how to ride."

My father had taught me to be stoic, to be "a man," but, in that moment, it took all my strength not to break down in pity and rage at how he had been mistreated. I had always been impressed by his strength and daring in sports, and it took on even greater meaning as I learned of his earlier trauma.

My mother suffered her share of emotional scars, too, including bouts of depression. We blamed it on the threats that came with life under Communism, combined with the psychological toll of WWII. After growing up like a princess in the idyllic hot-springs village, Buziaș, adjusting to deprivation was especially hard for her. Anyu, as we called her in Hungarian, often got distraught over the most trivial matters, from a rainy day to a bird flying into a window, and she would threaten to run off.

When she got "excited," as we called it, my father would slowly move to the door to make sure she didn't bolt. As a child, I didn't understand why she acted this way, but I obeyed when he told Gabriel and me to help him block the exit. It was as if she had to prove to herself that we would always be there to protect her. Sometimes I felt guilty when I ignored her more unreasonable requests, although they made it easier for me to distance myself from her. Now I suspect PTSD: the trauma of having to hide in the countryside to avoid German soldiers was still very fresh for her and must have contributed to her erratic behavior.

When I was growing up, there was no official source of reliable news. We didn't have a TV at home, and it was illegal to listen to the American-run Radio Free Europe, which broadcast to eastern European countries to give them hope. There was only the Communist newspaper, which was all propaganda, so no one read it. Our main source of information was the rumor mill.

We often heard disturbing stories about people being mistreated by the State, and the threat of the unexpected perpetually hovered in the background, but for years nothing terrible happened to my immediate family. Then, one day when I was thirteen, it hit us: My sixty-two-year-old maternal grandmother, Piroska, did not return from the market. When she was still missing at dinnertime, we reluctantly went to the police. They claimed they knew nothing. We had heard stories of people disappearing but not grandmothers!

We didn't know what to do. We knew *something* had happened because she would never have stayed away so long. For the next three weeks, we were desperate. We almost gave up hope. Finally, the Commies released her on the other side of town. She had no idea where she was. Luckily, a kind gentleman who found her weeping on a bench figured out where she lived and escorted her home. She was so traumatized she could hardly speak.

Growing Up in Timişoara

The next day she told us what had happened: Two plainclothes "detectives" accosted her. They were actually KGB agents who took her to the infamous KGB headquarters and locked her in solitary confinement with almost nothing to eat. She was refused any contact with her family. They kept asking her questions she didn't know how to answer. They interrogated her in Romanian, a language she barely knew. Like most people of her generation, she spoke Hungarian and German. I can only imagine how scared she was.

We never knew why the KGB kidnapped my grandmother, but we suspected our family was targeted because of a sinister incident that had occurred a short time earlier: In 1955, the government allowed limited free enterprise, so my mother started a small knitting shop. She eventually had some forty-five women working for her. Yarn wasn't commercially available, so my father would gather it in its raw state from nearby villages, bring it to be spun, and then take it to be dyed in yet another village—all on his bicycle—after his job at Electromotor ended.

One day, a man in his early forties walked into the shop. He wore the menacing dark-green uniform of the much-feared Romanian KGB with insignias on his epaulets indicating that he was an officer. The customers quickly disappeared. He greeted my mother with a smirk. "Hello, sister," he said.

Instantly, my mother felt faint. She knew that she had a half-brother from her father's extramarital affair but she had never met him. Could the man in the uniform be her long-lost half-sibling? We only knew that his mother had been one of the household servants in my mother's childhood home. After my grandfather's untimely death, when my mother was six, the family continued to pay the woman to support her and to maintain the family secret.

"I thought it would be nice to get together," the man said.

My mother was petrified. A high-ranking officer appearing in her shop was no coincidence. He clearly wanted some type of payoff. She was afraid to alienate him, so she agreed to pay him every time he entered the shop.

When the authorities banned free enterprise three years later, we had to close the yarn shop, but my mother's half-brother still demanded payments, which we couldn't afford. We suspected he thought we had more resources than we did, and he punished us for holding out on him by apprehending—and terrifying—my grandmother.

Incidents like these were common and seemingly arbitrary—and they fostered a sense of unease and anxiety that haunts me to this day.

With free enterprise outlawed, my father struggled to find employment and often did odd jobs like repairing tomato crates. From 1958 to 1963, he resorted to framing old photographs for families who lived in the countryside. He would knock on doors, offering his services, and then restore and frame the photos in a shop in Timișoara. Eventually, he started promoting his restoration work in the proletarian apartment blocks in Bucharest. It's hard to believe, but he made enough money this way to support us modestly.

Between 1955 and 1958 (the years when we had enough money), we bought a pig every December, as did most assimilated Jews. Dad brought us with him to the market, chose the size of the pig according to the amount of money we could spend, and then sent the animal to the butcher in a closed wooden crate. The next day, the four of us cycled to the butcher on the outskirts of town. Overweight, middle-aged, and clad in a bloody white apron, the butcher looked like a pig himself to me. He would chase the poor animal around the muddy backyard with a big knife and eventually corner it, throw himself on top of it, and slit its throat. His wife would hold the pan to catch the blood. Then we would spend the day helping him prepare sausages of various types—blood, liver, head cheese, etc. The main attraction for us kids was the *kolbasz*—a mostly meat sausage with sweet paprika and other typically Hungarian spices.

I was both fascinated and repulsed by the scene. But it was a relief to know that we would have plenty to eat. We would have food for the year from this 300- to 400-pound pig—bacon, sausage, ham, and fat for cooking. The pantry near the kitchen would be filled with all kinds of goodies! At night, Gabriel and I would raid it for sausage and salami.

Other years, there was no pig. Nor was there any refrigeration, just a tin container inside a wooden ice box in which we placed chunks of ice brought to the city on carts by local farmers. This had been one of my maternal grandfather's businesses in the 1920s. His workers would cut ice from frozen lakes, keep it in pits covered with hay, and sell it in Timișoara in spring and summer. Even in the mid-1960s, no one in Romania had refrigerators. As kids, we would run behind the horse- or oxen-drawn carts, trying to pick up shards of ice or stealing small pieces of it from the truck. Farmers also delivered unpasteurized milk every day. To get bread, you had to line up at the bakery at 5 or 6 a.m. If people saw a line, they joined it automatically and after, asked, "What are we waiting for?" When I returned to my old hometown over Easter weekend in 1980, I was shocked to find people still lining up for a few eggs or scallions.

Although appalled by the primitive killing of the pig, I still yearn for all the pork products I enjoyed during my childhood, from head cheese to pork rinds. When I came to New York, I was delighted to discover the Hungarian section of Yorkville, where I could get these high-cholesterol goodies from stores that, sadly, have all but disappeared. These days, Gabriel and I will sometimes drive to a rundown neighborhood in Passaaic, New Jersey, to a store called Kolbasz.com, to buy the provisions we loved as kids.

Again, nearly all of our friends and acquaintances were Hungarian Jews, but neither my parents nor my grandparents had strong religious beliefs. Although they were secular, and strongly identified as part of the educated, upper-class Hungarian community, they also felt an irreducible Jewish identity, too. Just as it remains for many American secular Jews today, Judaism was, for us, important in some indescribable but crucial way, something not connected to religion, or even strictly to one particular set of cultural habits—but *defining* in some crucial, if abstract, way. Our family and friends attended the Great Synagogue (*Sinagoga*

Cetate), a beautiful, imposing Neolog-rite synagogue that had been built in the Oriental style in 1865; it resembled the great synagogue in Oran, Algeria. One of the largest synagogues in Europe, it was a reform/conservative synagogue where women and men were separated but men did not have to wear a skull cap (*kippah*). Like most Jewish families we knew, we attended two or three times a year, on special occasions.

One such occasion was my Bar Mitzvah. It took place in August of 1958, at the Great Synagogue. I read a short text that I didn't understand at all but had learned through transliteration and memorization. I was now formally accepted into the exclusive men's club of the Jewish community. Rabbi Neuman, then a young maverick, prepared me for the event. He taught the Bible in a child-friendly way on Sundays, telling kids watered-down, easily understandable stories that introduced them to this important part of their Jewish heritage.

I went to my maternal grandmother's home for meals after services and after my Bar Mitzvah, where my family devoured a whole chicken—not that much food for six people! The celebration was discreet, both for monetary reasons and because it was best not to draw attention to being Jewish.

A few months later, my maternal grandparents received notification that they would be allowed to leave Romania. Families who lived together were permitted to leave together, which meant my ninety-year-old great-grandmother could emigrate with them. They had a beautiful apartment, which might have been a factor in their release. It was a difficult decision for them, because they had no idea if they would ever see us again. Still, we all knew that if they didn't seize this opportunity, there would be no second chance. (My grandmother's decision was also undoubtedly influenced by the fact that the emigration papers arrived just months after her kidnapping.)

Ultimately, my grandmother, my great-grandmother, and my step-grandfather, Leo, decided to emigrate to Israel. Leo and I had spent many wonderful days together, and he was a significant person in my childhood. It was therefore a painful goodbye and a big loss for my parents, Gabriel,

Growing Up in Timișoara

and me. I was heartbroken after Leo left. We felt it especially during holidays, which we had always spent together.

School became more of a challenge for me. Often my mind would wander. After several teachers complained that I had come in late or talked during class, the principal dragged me to the barbershop—as he did with all troublemakers—to have my hair sheared off. It happened twice. He stayed until the barber had shorn a wide strip of hair from my forehead to the back of my head. Then he left, knowing the barber would complete the task.

When I got home, Dad asked, "Well, what happened this time?"

"I was bored and sent a note to Patrichi," I replied. "I didn't think they saw me."

Mom took one glance at me and groaned, "Not again."

My parents knew how hard the repressive regime was for kids, so they didn't punish me.

I didn't excel in math or science, but I had a gift for languages. By fifteen, I had learned Hungarian (I'm Hungarian), Romanian (I lived in Romania and went to a Romanian school), Russian (compulsory from fifth grade on), Latin (compulsory), German (from my father's parents), and English. I had taken private English lessons twice a week from age eleven to fifteen, hoping that one day we would escape this horrible place. My teacher, Dr. Margaret Vágó, had been my mother's childhood English teacher. A girl named Ági took lessons with me. Unfortunately, she wasn't very attractive, but she was nice enough to meet me in the staircase of Dr. Vágó's apartment ten minutes before every class so I could brush up on the lessons. There was a bridge over the Bega Canal where the tram slowed down near our home, so, whenever I was running late, I would jump on it and ride three stops to my English teacher's house without buying a ticket.

My mother decided I should learn French, too, and took me to a family friend for lessons. His windowless one-room apartment was decorated with brocade and other fabrics on the walls, and on the

19

day we first came, he was heating an apple on his potbelly stove to create a pleasant aroma. He was also sick in bed and drinking tea. I sat down in a chair across from him, and he threw a French magazine at me. "Read it," he said. And that's how I started learning French. Fortunately, French being a Romance language, it wasn't as difficult as I had feared. I stopped after a few lessons because my parents could no longer afford it, but I got a taste of the language and some confidence that I could speak it. I never had another lesson in French, but I'm conversationally fluent.

In Romania, high school ended after eleventh grade. Unfortunately, I failed my final exams in math and physics, which meant I'd failed the baccalaureate exams. I would not be able to graduate. Even with passing grades, I would never have been allowed to attend a college or university because my family had applied to leave the country. My only option would have been to continue my studies in a technical school, which didn't interest me. That left me even more depressed and angry. Because we had applied to leave, our opportunities in Romania were restricted, but we had no promise that we would ever be allowed to emigrate. It was an infuriating catch-22.

I got a second chance to take my exams in August 1962, with a little help from a paid "friend" of my parents, who could ensure that I would pass. (If you had money in Romania, you could buy almost anything.) I should have spent the summer studying for the exams, but it was hard to focus when I felt so hopeless. Instead, this became my daily routine: My mother and brother would go to the beautiful new city pool at the edge of town with a few friends who had younger kids. (It was surrounded by sand—a major novelty in land-locked Timișoara.) As soon as they left, I would bike to the pool and camp out at the other end, keeping an eye on my mother and her friends. Around 4 or 5 p.m., when they started packing up to go home, I would jump on the bike and rush home before they got there. Mother would walk in to find me hunched over my math books. One day, happy to see me studying so hard, she put her hand affectionately on the back of my head ... and realized my hair was wet. There were no showers in our home, only a bathtub with hot water once a month; I had to confess. Still, I passed the math exam with a 5.85 out of 10—just high enough to earn my high school diploma. I still keep it locked in my safe in New York.

I was a bright kid, but between my short attention span and my fervent sense of rebellion against my dull, authoritarian teachers, no doubt suffering as much as I under the new regime, made it impossible for me to thrive in academics at that time.

The academically inclined kids from my graduating class went to universities to study architecture, medicine, and engineering. The lower achievers studied languages at humanistic universities. Those who couldn't get in anywhere else went to the Timișoara University of Agriculture. They were usually from poorer, uneducated families. Since I couldn't go to any university, I got a job as an assistant to a mechanic in the University of Agriculture, working as a laborer, with oily hands and greasy overalls. I made 600 *lei* a month—about $10—and gave it all to my parents.

Bridge became my salvation; it was evidence of my intellect. From age sixteen to eighteen, my mother encouraged me to start a bridge club with three of my brighter classmates. We met twice a month and took turns hosting, while our parents served coffee and cake. It seemed very grown-up, which made me feel proud. When we graduated, and my schoolmates went on to the better universities, we continued our bridge games until age eighteen, when we finally emigrated.

Sports were another escape for me—and a route to self-esteem, because I excelled at them with little effort. As a teenager, I played table tennis, soccer, and basketball. I began to ski at four, when we took a weeklong ski vacation. Getting to the ski slopes was a complex activity. We boarded a train at dawn for a four-hour ride to Caransebes; then took a horse-drawn cart from the station to the foot of Muntele Mic. From there, we rode ponies 5,000 feet up the mountainside, to an inn called

Bella Vista. We arrived at sunset and started skiing the next morning. There were no ski lifts, and since there were only about twenty to thirty skiers on the slope, the snow was nothing like the kind on the slopes here. It was six to eight feet, deep and untouched, so that our skis left foot-deep tracks with no possibility of maneuvering. The wooden skis of the 1950s were quite rudimentary, with leather-strap bindings so that, if your ski popped off your boot, it would careen downhill until it hit a tree, or a bush, or worse, another skier. There were many small accidents, but it was still fun.

When we couldn't afford a trip to Muntele Mic in the wintertime, my father invented the idea of "taxi skiing." Since there were practically no cars on the roads in Timișoara, he would hire a taxi for half a day to drive us to the suburbs—usually on the road to Arad—and have the cab pull us with a cord for a few kilometers. The snow on the roads was beaten down, so it worked well. In fact, it was more fun than skiing on the mountain with knee-deep snow and no ski lifts.

When private enterprise was briefly allowed in the mid-1950s, and our family had decent income, we took several memorable vacations. One of our parents had to manage the yarn shop, so they took turns vacationing with us. Around 1955, a polio epidemic descended, and getting out of the city was imperative. One summer, my father took us to the mountains; another summer, my mother brought us to the Black Sea resort of Mamaia. We had a summer holiday every summer that we could afford one.

In the summer of 1957 or '58, we took our bicycles to Predeal, a 10-hour trip by train, for a three-week vacation. The highlight was taking our bikes up-mountain to Brasov, the highest city along the train route, and riding downhill to Predeal for five or six hours, coasting through the woods on wonderful paved roads, with the wind blowing through our hair. The biggest challenge was that the freight-car attendant insisted we let the air out of the tires, under the pretext that the movement of the train would make the bikes unmanageable. My father had no choice but to slip the attendant a bill, to ensure that our bicycles would be returned untouched when we arrived. When the bribes got too large, he refused to pay, so we had to blow up the tires when we reached the top. Despite the annoyance, these were wonderful, carefree days. There was no danger of traffic because there were no cars. As we rode down the open road, with virgin forest on each side, I looked at my father and imagined that during those moments, he had recaptured some of the joy and hope of his youth. I truly felt was sharing that exhilarating feeling with us.

I took another memorable trip when I was sixteen and a half. On New Year's Eve, my old friend George Reisner and I visited my uncle Gyuri Wiener, a colonel in the Communist Army, at his home in Bucharest. Uncle Gyuri, my mother's younger brother, had dedicated his life to the Communist movement starting at age sixteen, largely because an older friend had convinced him to. Leo and my mother had tried to dissuade him, but to no avail. We rarely saw him, so this visit was a special treat.

Uncle Gyuri and his wife, Vera, went out for the evening and left us home with a radio and a bottle of cocoa liquor. I had never before tasted alcohol. I tried a few sips with George, who is two years older than I. Fueled by liquid courage, we decided to go out on the town.

"After all, we're in Bucharest," George pointed out.

"What should we wear?" I asked. I looked around and spied my uncle's military coat and hat with the colonel epaulets and all the appropriate insignias. "Perfect!"

George, older and wiser, tried to discourage me, but it seemed like a fun thing to do. My uncle was shorter and smaller than I was, but I squeezed eagerly into his clothes. "I'm ready," I announced. "Let's have fun!"

There was snow coming down and already several inches on the ground. We soon found ourselves near the Royal Palace, which had become the Communist Party Central Committee's building, and the seat of government. Officers were out in the street with their wives on their arms, celebrating New Year's Eve. A couple of them saluted me, and I saluted back with a serious expression.

George, who had been lagging behind me, caught up and told me in a terrified whisper that we should return home immediately. He'd just overheard an officer remarking to his wife: "What a young colonel. Interesting..."

I acquiesced, and we hurried back to the small, drab apartment, which was safe but dull. Only in retrospect did I realize how lucky I was not to be arrested for what would have been a serious offense under Communist rule.

A short time later, George and his family got their exit visa. I thought I would never see him again. Looking back, I realize that donning my uncle's uniform and flouting authority was my way of fending off despair. We had no guarantee that we would ever be given permission to emigrate. No one knew how families were selected. It was like winning the lottery. *What if we never win?* I asked myself. *What if we're stuck here forever?*

3
Israel

*F*ive grueling years dragged by since my grandparents' departure for Israel. We kept telling ourselves it would be our turn soon, but it was hard not to give up hope.

In the '50s, there were rumors that you could leave Romania if you had a Western entry visa. Excited at the prospect, we managed to obtain an entry visa to Nicaragua through my mother's cousins, who had emigrated there before WWII. I still remember the large, colorful engraved document festooned with ribbons and stamps. Unfortunately, the authorities were not impressed. We were stuck in Romania.

Then, at long last, a year after my graduation from high school, my mother, father, my father's mother, Gabriel, and I received the papers to emigrate in July of 1963! We never knew whether my uncle's position in the Communist Party had delayed or expedited our departure. Since he had committed to the party, he no longer had the option to leave.

We later heard that Jewish organizations in the West were paying the Romanian government thousands of dollars per capita to release Jews who had requested exit visas. Perhaps that was the driving force behind our visas. Romania was home to more than 350,000 Jews after

THE LAST IMPRESARIO

WWII (the Soviet Union was the only other European country with a larger Jewish population), and the country's economic picture was bleak indeed, so a cash-for-exit-visas strategy would certainly have appealed to the government. According to the rumor mill, the Communists delayed sending young people who could help the Jewish state but eagerly sent older ones, who would be a burden to it.[1]

As we soon discovered, getting our visas was just the beginning of our odyssey. Leaving Romania proved to be a traumatic experience. To give you a final humiliating kick in the ass—and as a reminder that we were at their mercy—the government forced you to paint and fix up your apartment—and then give it to the State, instead of selling it. Because you had to hire government-appointed painters for an outrageous price, you had to sell your few material possessions and get loans from family, friends, and the Jewish community to afford the upgrades. To make matters worse, the apartment had to pass inspection by the authorities before they would accept it.

Nonetheless, my father was in such a hurry to leave that he immediately liquidated most of our meager belongings, and we were on our way in less than two weeks. I gave my record player to a friend, since I couldn't bring much with me. At that time, the government was forcing people to leave Romania by plane, though we were able to skirt this rule because my grandmother was emigrating with us, and her health was too poor for air travel.

The night before we left, I couldn't sleep. My father was as excited as I was. "Our nightmare is almost over, Petruska'm," he said, using one of his favorite nicknames for me.

Not quite. The train ride was nerve-wracking because there were armed police looking everywhere for stowaways and scrutinizing our papers at every stop. We passed guard posts flanked by barbed-wire fences, knowing there probably were landmines under the wire. Our first stop was Budapest, but only for an hour, so we were afraid to venture far from the train. When we crossed the border from Hungary to Austria, leaving the barbed wire behind, I saw tears in my father's eyes for the first time in my life. We were finally free! A monumental step! What irony that we gained our freedom in Austria, home of the Nazis.

With my father and Gabriel

My grandmother experienced it differently. She was so traumatized by leaving her home of sixty-plus years that she could barely speak. She slept for most of the trip, and during the rare moments when she was awake, she seemed off in space.

I remember asking her, "Aren't you happy that we are finally going to Israel? Now we have an opportunity to start a new life!"

My grandmother did not reply.

She was at the end of her life. In retrospect, I realize that for her, our journey meant leaving everything behind. Meanwhile, I had just turned eighteen. For me, endless possibilities lay ahead.

When we reached the Vienna Hauptbahnhof, my father's cousin, Edith Dornhelm, was waiting with her husband, Bandi, to give us a warm welcome. Edith was my favorite aunt and my mother's best friend. They had known each other as young women and been pregnant at the same time in 1945. Edith gave birth two weeks after I was born, and both women named their boys "Peter." My "younger" cousin Peter and I were fairly close during childhood but had seen each other only a few times since then. Their family had emigrated about five years earlier, after Bandi's release from prison. He had been sentenced for several years for hiding a portion of his family's jewelry rather than surrendering it to the authorities.

We stayed with the Dornhelms in Vienna for three days before flying to Tel Aviv. One of the highlights of our visit was an amusement park with go-carts and a Ferris wheel—a small one, but my first, so for me, it was a fantasy. The other highlight was that my "uncle" Bandi gave me my first taste of whiskey. After one sip, I got a headache. (It was only in my early thirties that I began to develop a taste for wine.)

After our brief respite, we continued on to Israel. The first time I set foot on a plane was in mid-August 1963 for the trip from Vienna to Tel Aviv, after carrying my grandmother through the airport. We landed in Israel in the early evening. I remember the hot, humid, tropical air hitting me as I stepped off the plane. It was something I had never experienced—a new world, with palm trees, tropical vegetation, and exotic Middle Eastern buildings. I had promised myself that I would kiss the ground upon arrival, but the hot, oily runway deterred me. Instead, I put 1 knee down as a symbol of my devotion to the land of my ancestors.

Local officials welcomed us, and, within a short time, we were reunited with my grandparents. I was overjoyed to see Leo again and couldn't get enough of his company. But I soon saw that he was a fish out of water in Israel. He and my grandmother were only in their sixties and seventies, but they seemed old and frail. In those days, middle-aged women wore long dark clothes and avoided makeup. They looked like they were preparing to die. Older immigrants had an especially hard time learning Hebrew, which bears no resemblance to any European language. It struck me as an apt metaphor for the culture shock many of them must have felt. Here they were in their historic homeland, unable to speak their mother tongue. Their children had to teach them or translate for them.

We spent a few days with my grandparents in their home at Rehov Tabor 6 in the village of Kfar Ata, near Haifa. Then we moved to one

Israel

of the asbestos shacks the Jewish Agency for Israel provided for new immigrants—#118B in the Amidar B development.

It was depressing and basic, but, still, we were free and in our own land, where "our" language was spoken. (Ironically, none of us spoke it!) This 600-square-foot shack would be our home for the next several months. It had a 10 foot by 8 foot living room and two similarly sized bedrooms. A solar panel on the roof provided intermittent hot water.

My grandparents introduced Gabriel and me to several young people who were near my age, and we went to a few Friday-night parties. The highlight was always slow dancing to Paul Anka, Elvis, and Cliff Richard. On Saturdays, enterprising drivers who used flatbed trucks to transport goods during the week turned their vehicles into makeshift buses in which they transported young people to the beach, a dangerous way to travel. The beach was a rather primitive environment, with no food stand, running water, or changing cabanas. We had no sunscreen, and I remember burning to a crisp several times. In the evening, the big attraction was going to the only movie house in Kfar Ata, to see the only film playing. It was there that I saw *West Side Story*, two years after its release. It portrayed a world that felt very far away. After a few weeks, like most young immigrants to Israel, the Jewish Agency Sochnut assigned me to Kibbutz Kfar Blum, which was located in northern Galilee, a few hundred yards from the Syrian border.

The kibbutz was supposed to help me master Hebrew, and get acclimated to Israeli society. It was the first time I had been away from my parents and Gabriel. I was so overwhelmed with everything that was happening in my life that I felt homesick only a few weeks into my time there. The kibbutz was a fascinating experience. The new foods, the scents, the beautiful countryside, and the sense of community all engaged me. The daily routine required rising at 5 a.m. and working from 6 to noon, when the sun reached its high point. Lunch in the mess hall was a salad of chopped tomatoes and cucumbers, some yogurt, vegetables, and meat. I collected garbage, cleaned chicken coops, drove a tractor, and picked apples. The hardest and most unpleasant job was moving fifteen-foot irrigation pipes through cornfields with stalks ten feet high. We balanced the pipes with both hands, but the leaves of the stalks would hit our arms and shoulders, dropping pollen onto our sweaty skin and making it itch like hell. One of my vivid memories is spending an hour in a concrete shelter during a mock attack by the Syrian army, which was stationed in the hills above Kibbutz Kfar Blum.

Although by then, I spoke several languages, Hebrew proved a major challenge. Lots of young people spoke English or Romanian, so I didn't have to speak Hebrew to communicate, which further slowed my learning. It took me almost three years to really master the language of our ancestors.

After five months on the kibbutz, I was ready to leave, despite the expectation that we would stay for six months in the process of making *Aliya*, or "returning home" to Israel. It was December by then, cold and damp, and I'd been assigned to outdoor labor.

Our teacher, Rivka, encouraged me to stay. "Why leave now?" she asked. "You've made nice progress."

"I'm sure I'll find my way," I replied, putting on a brave front. "I must try something new." There was no question in my mind that seeking the unknown was worth the risk, but I was secretly terrified.

In spite of very limited money and means of communication, Gabriel and I managed to see each other a few times during the five months I spent at Kfar Blum. Gabriel had finished ninth grade in Romania, so he was sent to Lohamei HaGetaot, a kibbutz established by the survivors of the Warsaw ghetto, to continue his high school education.

On my way back to my parents' asbestos shack, I stopped by to see him. Gabriel, with other young immigrants his age, was having his first exposure to Hebrew and Israeli society. One of the most emotional memories I have is being reunited with Gabriel in a banana orchard, with oversized leaves moving in the tropical breeze, something I had never seen before. I was also pleased to have this private time with Gabriel.

Israel

With Gabriel

In the summer of 1964, our family moved to Holon, a southern suburb of Tel Aviv, and Gabriel enrolled in the local high school with less-than-perfect Hebrew but highly determined to succeed. He graduated in June 1967, during the all-consuming events of Israel's Six Day War.

After completing high school, Israeli graduates usually start their compulsory military service, unless they are admitted to a special program. Gabriel successfully completed the admission test to the Technion, Israel's prestigious Institute of Technology, in Civil Engineering. After, he was accepted to the *Atuda* program, in which recruits spent four years attaining an engineering degree and completing the military training required to become combat officers. Early on, Gabriel knew that he wanted to be a civil engineer like our Uncle Gyuri. I, on the other hand, despite being the older child, felt lost. No traditional profession appealed to me. During the endless bus ride to my parents' shack that rainy December day, I contemplated my future, as murky as the drops beating down on the window.

I was in a dark mood as my bus approached the dreary Haifa bus station. I took yet another local bus to my parents' asbestos shack in Kfar-Ata. They were as lost as I, despite having reconnected with some old friends from Timișoara. The changes were overwhelming for all of us, but it was hardest for them. They had no higher education, no influential contacts, and no money. They didn't know how to get started. My mother took some courses in Hebrew, learned enough to communicate basics, and got a job as a waitress. My father didn't even try to learn the language. He eventually got a job as an accountant at a hotel restaurant. Despite the low level of these positions similar to most of their peers from back home, my parents were still pleased to begin a new life in Tel Aviv with old friends from Timișoara. In two years, they were able to save enough money to buy a two-bedroom apartment at 94 Hayarkon Street. It was in the heart of Tel Aviv and a lovely place that overlooked the Mediterranean.

I was grateful that my parents were relatively content with their new life. I knew, though, that they were in no position to offer me emotional or financial support. I would have to figure things out on my own. A few days after I left Kfar Blum, I got a job as a laborer at the ATA textile factory and worked for the next seven months, earning a basic salary. After that, at the suggestion of a family friend, and with no other, more-appealing options, I started hotel training. It seemed to be somewhat glamorous, worldly work in which being multilingual would be an asset and where I might even make my mark.

After ten months of hotel training at the Tadmor Hotel School in Herzliah, near Tel Aviv, I got my first hotel job. It was in Tiberias on the lake of Galilee, just under the Golan Heights, which was still in Syrian hands. At nineteen, I was independent for the first time, earning reasonable money and enjoying disposable income. I rented a car to explore the Northern Galilee countryside, ate well, and taught myself to waterski.

Intrigued by the nuances of each culture I encountered, I carefully observed how American and European tourists dressed, spoke, and behaved. I enjoyed starting conversations with them, during which I improved my command of their languages and learned more about them as people. What did they think of Israel? Which tourist sites appealed to them? How did they find the food here, as compared to their own? I wanted to know everything.

My dad came to visit me in Tiberias and waterskied with me, which reminded me of our old holidays in Romania. Still quite athletic, he had no trouble getting up on the skis. Watching him, I felt both impressed and touched. I was particularly pleased that I was now able to introduce him to something new and that, now, it was *my* treat.

After a year and a half in provincial Tiberias, I got a job at the front desk of the historic King David Hotel in Jerusalem. It was a plum job, where I dealt with an affluent international clientele. I had more opportunity to use my languages than I'd had in remote Tiberias, and I had more contact with Americans. They awoke my curiosity about life in the U.S., something I could hardly even contemplate or imagine a few years earlier.

America! The land of opportunity! I had met several American teenagers and been impressed by their confidence and the exciting life they described in the States. Nearby, I had rented a pearl of a studio apartment on Ben Yehuda street, with a large terrace and a grand view overlooking the old city from the twelfth floor. I comfortably settled in at the King David front desk for more than a year and a half.

And then another seismic change occurred. At that time, a melancholy mood had descended on the country, despite Israel's great victory in the Six Day War. Most of us knew that the armed struggle with our neighbors was not over. Fear caused tourism to come to a halt. I felt it was time to spread my wings, and, with my parents' encouragement, I decided to train at a hotel school in Switzerland. I decided that first I would work in Cologne or Vienna in order to improve my German before using it in an academic setting.

I knew that this departure was exceedingly painful for my parents, who, aware of my need for adventure, sensed that it might be permanent. Despite their grief, they embraced my decision, even coming to see me off.

THE LAST IMPRESARIO

You weren't allowed to leave Israel with more than $400 in cash, but I had managed to save $1,150, so a friend of my parents designed a penholder that would conceal the money. We attached the penholder to a letter from my parents that read, "Dear Petrushkam, please write. We are anxious to hear how you are doing . . . ," so that the pen case would look like a gift.

At dusk on December 18, 1967, I embarked on the Greek-owned *Stella Solaris*—a modest, medium-sized ship—for the voyage to Crete and on to Genoa. All I had in my pocket was a reference from the King David to the manager of the Sheraton Hotel on Park Ave. in New York City, as unlikely as I thought it was that I'd need it.

4
There Would Be Music

I gazed out at the Haifa port from the deck of the *SS Stella Solaris*. The sun was setting, and I felt a chill in my bones. It was mid-December of 1967, and the Mediterranean was stormy. I felt lonely and unsettled as I started my voyage, but I desperately wanted to expand my horizons. I hoped this journey would give me a direction and a focus that could sustain my interest. I didn't yet realize that I had attention deficit disorder (ADD), but I knew that I got bored and distracted easily. What could possibly change that?

The *Solaris* was filled with couples and families, but I had a decent single cabin. I was fascinated by the duty-free shops' cashiers, who could convert prices of duty-free items among different European currencies quickly. Everything else was misty, like the sea. I was emotionally exhausted from contemplating what lay ahead, but also excited to see new sights, especially in Cyprus and Greece. I had passed the test to get a driver's license in Israel, so I rented a Vespa in Crete. I nearly killed myself trying to ride it. Covered in bruises and scrapes, I hobbled back to the *Solaris* just before it set sail for Italy.

THE LAST IMPRESARIO

When we arrived in Genoa, I was elated to find that I could understand most of the signs and menus despite never having studied the language. I had knowledge of both Latin and French, and this proved enough for me to at least decipher basic signage. Speaking the language, however, was not nearly as easy. I found a $5 hotel for the night, and the next day, I made my way to the train station to purchase a ticket to Florence. I wanted to see the Renaissance treasures that I'd seen in my grandfather's art books.

When I stepped out of the station, I felt as though I had landed on another planet. Florence had just begun its recovery from the 1966 flood that had compromised its infrastructure and destroyed much of its art. Still, the city's grandeur overwhelmed me. The open holiday celebration hit me hard, and the seasonal decorations, in particular, struck at my heart. I knew this was a Catholic country, but an open celebration of Christmas was still hard for me to grasp. There are, of course, churches in Timişoara, but under Communism, open displays of religion were strongly discouraged. Decorations were minimal and used only inside houses of prayer. Also, electricity was so costly that the streets were always dark. (Even in 1996, when I returned, there were no lights on the road from Hungary.) At any rate, the commercial aspect of the holiday was entirely new to me.

The narrow streets of Florence were incredibly beautiful. But it was cold and rainy, and I had little money, no guidebook, and no sense of where to turn. It was hard to tour the city alone in those conditions, and I began to miss my family and to yearn for anything familiar. After two days, I was ready to leave. I planned to take a train to Vienna, where my Aunt Edith and her husband, the same relatives who had hosted us when we left Romania, were expecting me.

I was determined to visit Milan first to see La Scala and the Duomo. They were two places I had dreamed of since I was a little boy, studying my grand- father's art books. Like Florence, Milan was decked with lights and pine wreaths and countless nativity scenes for the holiday. I had never seen such an abundance of decorations or witnessed such collective joy.

There Would Be Music

It permeated the air. Lovers strolled past arm in arm, and small children scampered gaily about while their parents trailed behind, carrying packages wrapped in red and green. The tiny shops that lined the streets and the cozy corner restaurants beckoned to passersby.

Milan at Christmas was breathtaking, but I felt I had no place in it, that I didn't belong. I reflected on my earlier exposure to this world—Grandpa Eugene's beautifully bound art books filled with pictures of Italian Renaissance masterpieces, the countless imaginary voyages I had made to the mysterious and faraway West with those books in hand, the world I longed to be a part of. But it was one thing to read and pretend; it was quite another to sit here in a cafe alone. I felt as if I were in a dream. It was hard to believe any of it was real.

I sat down and ordered a cappuccino from a tuxedo-clad waiter. I'd never tasted a cappuccino and had no idea what to expect. Cappuccinos had not yet come to Israel by 1967, and, before that, I had lived in a drab, colorless Communist country. The foam seemed an almost surreal flourish. Equally bizarre was the waiter's attire. He was dressed in clothes I had seen only in my parents' art books and wedding photos. Why should someone who served cappuccino be dressed this way? It made no sense.

The cappuccino was delicious, and it briefly warmed the chill that had enveloped me, soothed the raw feelings within. I savored it as I watched the passersby. I thought of my father and his determination to maintain his dignity, no matter what circumstances he found himself in. Even though I felt entirely out of place, I tried not to show it. Casually, I picked up an Italian newspaper to see if I could understand it. I remembered my father's words: "Don't just look, *see!*" He wanted me to be able to describe in detail what I observed, whether it was the petals of a flower or the caryatids of a great church.

It was hard to take in all the nuances of this world, from the formality of the waiters to the grandeur of the buildings. I was lonely, and as I had no winter coat, quite cold.

THE LAST IMPRESARIO

I spent the afternoon drifting around a frigid Milan, trying to navigate the city's winding *strade* and impressive *piazze*, using the little Italian I knew. I had wandered from the Piazza del Duomo through the Galleria Vittorio Emanuele II, the elite shopping arcade of Milano. It was three days until Christmas, and the streets were filled with people. Entering the square, a jovial couple about to duck into a small bistro approached me and spoke rapidly in Italian. They seemed to be inviting me for a drink, but I felt shy and awkward. I managed to decline and continued walking as they entered the bar. Then they suddenly turned back to wish me, *"Buon Natale!"*

At that moment, I caught sight of what I'd been searching for. There she stood, directly across from me. La Scala.

Daylight was fading quickly, and as I hurried across the piazza, snowflakes began to fall. I approached the stately opera house eagerly, hoping to go inside, but the doors had closed only moments before. With nothing else to do and nowhere to be, I stood at the entrance, staring at the building's façade.

Here was my childhood dream. I could touch it, feel the cold, imposing stone of its exterior. But there was no way inside, which seemed fitting. I was a stranger in a strange land, and La Scala was beyond my reach. Standing there shivering in the cold, I felt convinced that the music had eluded me. I thought about the idealization of the opera when I was a child. My parents owned an RCA gramophone. After dinner and on quiet Sunday afternoons, my father would wind up the beautiful old phonograph, a gift from my grandfather, and we would all sit in the living room reading or playing chess and listening to Tchaikovsky, Dvořák, Prokofiev. How we idealized the world from which that music came!

Music meant a great deal to us in those bleak post-World War II days behind the Iron Curtain. It was a reminder of the beauty and freedom these impoverished countries had enjoyed before the devastation of war and the subsequent Communist regime. My father would tell Gabriel and me stories of our charming little town of Timișoara before the Soviets took over. He would fall into a reverie as he remembered the personal freedom he had enjoyed, his entrepreneurial successes, and the happy, bourgeois existence he and my mother had briefly lived when they married. They had hoped to enjoy it for a lifetime.

Of all the LPs my parents owned—and they had quite a collection—my favorite by far was the nine-piece vinyl set of Antonin Dvořák's *Symphony from the New World*. I remember sitting on the frayed rug in my grandparents' cramped living-room floor as a boy, savoring one movement after the next. The music enthralled me. There was so much suspense in the sound, the swell and crescendo of the strings, the rumble of the drums, the mere velocity of the music. Every time I listened to it, I imagined stories of heroic escape, stories of adventure and conquest, stories in which the good guys vanquished the bad in bloody battles. What did it mean, this "New World"? Was it real? And if so, how could I get there? Dvořák's music conjured a world so exciting, so magical, so full of hope. And yet this world and all that it promised had felt impossibly, painfully out of reach. The idealization of the unknown was palpable.

Opera also had a special place in my heart as a child, thanks to my grandmother, Piroska, whom we called *Naci*. She wasn't affable or coddling in a conventional grandmotherly way, but she was a formidable baker and nurtured my weakness for sweets at a young age. She also encouraged my love of music and opera. At the time, her upstairs neighbor was the well-known soprano Ica Mavrodin, the local diva at the Timișoara opera house. When I was eight, Naci took me to see *Carmen* and *Peter and the Wolf*. I was mesmerized by the beauty of the production, the costumes, the lighting, and the music. After the performance, she took me to congratulate Ica and to meet her fellow actors. I still remember sitting backstage while *Naci* visited with Ica, watching the sweaty and extravagantly made-up performers, the elaborate costumes, and the beautifully constructed set up close. It was the very inverse of the drab world outside, and it was magic.

As twilight descended on that frosty December evening, I stood outside the locked doors of the grand opera house alone with my thoughts, never dreaming that there would be music—a great deal of beautiful music—in my future.

5
The New World Awaits

*I*taly had left me yearning for the comfort of family, so I was particularly eager for my visit with Aunt Edith. Although I hadn't seen her since August of 1963, when my family and I were on our way to Israel, I remembered the beauty of Vienna, the gardens, the enticing meals, and the summer days I had enjoyed during my brief stay. Exhausted and chilled, I took a bus to Milan's Stazione Centrale. There were no kiosks, only a long line snaking back from a single ticket booth. I joined it instinctively, an old habit from my days in Romania. Using my broken Italian, I struggled to make myself understood enough to purchase a second-class ticket; then I waited in the lounge for warmth until it was time to board the next train to Vienna. The trip was uneventful, and I was too overwhelmed with new sights and sensations to process more, so I slept for a good part of it.

On my first visit to Vienna, I had been in a dreamlike state. Having just left Communism, everything had a rose tint to it. Returning alone now, in December, things were quite different. No one was there to meet me at the train station, since my relatives didn't know when my train was due to arrive. I found a phone booth, called Aunt Edith, and got directions from her to give the taxi driver. My relatives were glad to see me, but to my surprise, I felt awkward. Italy had left me homesick, and Vienna was not *home*. Nor was it the warm, sunlit place I remembered. Much to my disappointment, winter here was harsh, windy, and unwelcoming—the weather seemed to reflect the city's attitude toward me.

I spent two weeks trying to find a job, and Aunt Edith did all she could to help, but I had no success. I was out of sync with the formality of the city, particularly the fine hotels, despite my time working at the King David in Jerusalem. Although I spoke German, my vocabulary was limited, and I didn't feel comfortable with the language or the environment. After New Year's Eve in 1968, I decided to move on to Cologne, where my mother's first cousin Leslie Wiener and his wife, Illy, lived with their son, Andreas, seven years my junior. Leslie had been like an uncle and Andy like a younger brother to me growing up. They had left Romania around the same time we did and were fairly established in Cologne now. Always a role model for me, Leslie worked as a mechanical engineer at Ford Germany and, being enterprising, he constructed electric billboards as a sideline through his own company, which he called Electrolicht. I remember him carrying them on a ski rack to sell the idea.

Within a week of arriving in Cologne, I got a desk position at the prime Frankfurter Hoff in Frankfurt. I found the hotel too formal and my colleagues unfriendly. I managed to transfer to the Dom Hotel, a relatively small, elegant, old-fashioned hotel near the famous Cologne cathedral. But it too was rigid and stifling after working in Israel, which was less formal—a quality that appealed to me immensely after the restrictive Communist regime in Romania. The only upside of my new job was that it allowed me to practice my German.

Meanwhile, I had begun dating a tall, pretty girl of 18. She was playful and flirtatious, and I enjoyed spending time with her, but it became clear she was not looking for the same kind of relationship I was. Both my work and my social life were big disappointments. I began missing the warm weather and blue skies of Israel—and my immediate family—more than ever. Still, I longed for adventure.

The New World Awaits

My thoughts turned to America. I had met Americans in Israel who said the U.S. offered opportunities for foreigners. They described it as an open, multi-ethnic society, free from the rigid class distinctions so prevalent in Germany. After Uncle Leslie and Andy took a trip to the U.S. in the spring of 1968 and came back raving about it, I decided it was time to see for myself. When I broached the subject with my parents, they suggested I contact distant relatives of ours in New York. I barely knew them, much less felt that I could depend on them, but I decided to take the risk anyway. I was twenty-three years old, with $200 to my name. I spent $95 of it on a one-way charter ticket to New York City.

I landed at JFK International Airport in August of 1968, managed to find a bus, and headed straight to the Port Authority. There, I caught another bus to Piscataway, New Jersey, where my mother's friends lived. Drs. Adrienne and Leslie Krausz and their twenty-one-year-old daughter, Marietta, welcomed me to their home, a rambling four-bedroom mansion in a tranquil neighborhood filled with winding, tree-lined roads and chirping birds. There were push-button phones and two Cadillacs parked in the garage, which was opened with a remote control.

Adrienne and Leslie were also hosting their French cousin, Peter, and his American girlfriend, Ellen Rounseville. From the moment Ellen and I saw each other, there were sparks. One night she stole quietly into my room while I was sleeping. I was awakened by her delicate hand touching my forehead. She whispered, "May I join you?" I thought it might be a dream. America was already seeming more like the Promised Land than Israel ever had.

Although Ellen was the one who changed romantic partners under the Krauszes' roof, they were understandably furious with me. I knew that I had behaved badly, but Ellen was impossible to resist after my having been alone for some time. I was eager to start looking for work in New York anyway, so I apologized and left. Ellen came with me. We spent the next few days at the rat- and roach-infested St. James Hotel in

Times Square, quite a contrast to the manicured lawns of New Jersey. In a few days, we rented a studio apartment at 1354 1st Avenue.

At my parents' suggestion, I contacted my mother's relatives, two Hungarian grand dames named Carrie Gody, whom we called *Schatzi*, and Marta Kleyman, whom we knew as *Maki*. My grandmother had raised them after their own mother died, and they were like older sisters to my mother. Both women had married and, as the clouds of war in Europe gathered in the 1930s, tried to emigrate to America. They were refused entry and headed to Nicaragua instead, but managed to move to New York a few years later. Both were affluent, successful, and glamorous. They reminded me of Zsa Zsa Gabor, with their flamboyant manner and the way they called everyone "*dahling!*"

Maki suggested I meet with Maia, her daughter, who was an artist. Maia and her husband—a fellow Transylvanian named John Farber, a self-made multi-millionaire—lived with their four children in a luxurious apartment at River House on East 52nd Street. I was overwhelmed when Maia proudly showed me around their home. Each child had a bedroom *and* a playroom. The apartment seemed never-ending. Here was a relative of mine with a very similar background and family history who was living in a veritable palace. I was hoping for a helping hand, hoping she would say, "Hey, stay with us for a while . . ." Instead, she offered me a glass of water with ice, *plenty* of ice.

Proudly presenting my handwritten reference to HR at the Park Avenue Sheraton, I was disappointed that they had no openings, but they did suggest I contact the Central Park Sheraton. By the end of August, I'd landed my first American job, as a night auditor at the Central Park Sheraton on Seventh Avenue and 55th Street. Since I couldn't work on a tourist visa, human resources arranged a one-year internship "to train me." Now twenty-three, I had a job in America, a job that paid in *dollars*. Granted, it only paid $95 a week but dollars nonetheless, while my weekly rental at the St. James Hotel on 45th Street was only $25.50. I was ecstatic.

The New World Awaits

One day in October, Tom Riley, the front-desk manager of the Wellington Hotel, which is across the street from the Central Park Sheraton, walked in, looking for someone to help out a few times a week. I jumped at the opportunity to earn more money, unaware that my visa prohibited other gainful employment. I also started researching ways to advance my hotel career and enrolled in a course at the American Hotel Management Association. At the same time, I started taking courses at Baruch College in American literature, logic, and introductory law. To help pay for the courses, I started driving a taxi in my spare time. My days were full, but I was able to work, pay for school, and save some money for travel.

I hired an immigration lawyer named Stephen Mukamal to help me get a U.S. labor permit that would convert into a Green Card. Steve explained that, to get approval, I would need an employer to prove that he or she couldn't find an American to meet their requirements.

My cousin Kitty, daughter of Schatzi, owned an import/export company called Kitkat. She created a position that required someone who spoke Hungarian, Romanian, Russian, Hebrew, French, and German. As required by law, she advertised in three states. When no one responded, she was able to offer me the job. This provided me a labor permit, which, in turn, allowed me to apply for a Green Card.

I had met Kitty once before coming to New York—when she visited my mother in Israel—but she embraced me as family. She was an extraordinary woman, and she played a pivotal role in my early days in New York.

Kitty was one of the first women to have a seat on the NY Stock Exchange. By the time I met her, she was an avid art collector and a friend of major artists like Larry Rivers, Robert Rauschenberg, and Alexander Calder, whom she had enlisted to design hammocks, woven in Nicaragua, with his initials.

She had an exceptional sense of design. She was profiled in a style magazine as the first person to create a loft-like space so that her bedroom would have views of Central Park. *What a concept! In the big city, you can even have your bed in the living room.* It seemed that in America you could challenge the rules—even rewrite them—without any consequences and with great rewards as well.

Kitty always made me feel included, whether we were at an auction house or the Hampton Classic, and I responded to her passion, creativity, and commitment to family. She was constantly changing her environment and buying up grand properties around the world, from Mayfair in London to a SoHo loft to a country house in Punta d'Este as well as a property in Lima, Peru. Her outrageously flamboyant style was contagious—when you were around her, you started to feel that life was brimming with opportunity. Dinner for twenty at the drop of a hat? Buying at auction? Why not? The possibilities seemed endless—and all within reach. In 1983, Kitty suggested I buy a very provocative Rauschenberg collage for $800,000. Unfortunately, I didn't have the funds. Now it's worth millions. Kitty would have found a way to buy it. That was how she lived her life. When she believed in something, she went for it. Of course, there were risks, but Kitty was a visionary. She was also a wonderful role model for me. She believed life was an adventure and that success would come.

I remember sitting in her grand sunroom on Gin Lane in Southampton, discussing the fall of the Berlin Wall with her. "Why didn't I realize this was inevitable?" she remarked. "It would have been a great time to buy property in Eastern Europe."

Kitty moved easily around the world but was also devoted to her family. I am still very fond of her two children, with whom I spent a good amount of time. I recall once taking Eric to Chinatown, where we bought toy swords and dueled in the streets. I also taught Risa how to ride her bike in Central Park, which was just across the street from Kitty's apartment on 59th Street. My relationship to them as young children meant a great deal to me, especially because I had no immediate family nearby.

Kitty might have been self-involved, but during my early days in New York, I knew I could count on her. She would come through if I really needed her—and, as it turned out, I did.

The New World Awaits

Ellen and I continued living together. She was lively, quick-witted, and seductive, but I felt she was also emotionally detached, struggling to define herself. In spite of our deep affection for each other, we were unable to support each other. In retrospect, I was too overwhelmed by my own challenges to be sympathetic to hers.

In the meantime, I had gotten to know Annie, the daughter of the general manager at the Park Sheraton, who lived in her father's suite on the top floor of the hotel. Our relationship was nothing more than a mildly flirtatious friendship, but the head of human resources, who had given me my first job in the U.S., misinterpreted it. He thought I was dating Annie, and he was furious.

"You shouldn't mix business and pleasure, young man!" he warned. "This could compromise your job."

One day, he called me into his office to forbid my relationship with Annie. But at the time, I was so enraged that I didn't bother to tell him our relationship was platonic. How dare he tell me what to do? This is the New World, and things were going well for me here. I wouldn't be working at this night job much longer, anyway. I had become cocky—a little too cocky, as it turned out.

By January 1969, I had saved enough money to take my first trip to the Caribbean, a fantasy of beautiful women and palm trees swaying in tropical breezes as I lounged in my hammock on the beach. I stopped at four islands—Haiti, Aruba, Curacao, and Puerto Rico—for two days each and then took a flight from San Juan to JFK. I had a wonderful time. I breezed through Immigration and Customs in Puerto Rico and, after my brief extravaganza, returned to work at the Sheraton and at my second job at the Wellington Hotel. Meanwhile, I had no idea that a one-year training visa did not allow for leaving the United States.

Most likely, the head of HR must have contacted the INS as a kind of retribution for my spending time with a woman he also liked. Two months later, at 4 a.m. on a rainy night in March of 1969, two immigration officers approached me at the front desk of the Wellington. "Are you Peter Klein?" they asked. Before I had a chance to answer, one of them showed me the gun under his belt. "Don't even think of running." He told me he was from the INS. "You're working this job illegally," he said. "You need to come with us." He handcuffed me, patted me down, and shoved me into the back seat of a two-door sedan. The agent climbed in the passenger seat and kept a wary eye on me as his fellow INS agent at the wheel pulled away from the curb.

They drove me to the Immigration holding facility in lower Manhattan, opening the car door only after the gate in the underground garage closed, and marched me into a large room with about fifty other detainees—mostly Chinese, whom I heard had jumped off ships and swum to New York Harbor. It was so crowded there weren't enough chairs for everyone. The hours crept by until 9:00 a.m., when I was given a dime and allowed to make my one phone call. I called Steve Mukamal, my lawyer. At noon, officers escorted me to a conference room, where Steve was waiting with an immigration judge named Greenberg. In spite of my anxiety, I remember being struck that there were three Jews in the room. What a nice change from the anti-Semitic atmosphere in old Romania. I felt a little reassured.

"So, young man, you're from Israel," said Judge Greenberg, whom I guessed was in his sixties.

"Yes, sir."

"You come to America, and you break the law by working two jobs," he said. "On the other hand, you're hardworking and enterprising."

"Thank you, sir."

"Then you break the law again by leaving the country while your lawyer is hard at work for you and sneaking back in through Puerto Rico."

"I'm so sorry, sir. I didn't know it was illegal for me to leave the country," I told him. "I had no idea it was wrong."

At this point, the judge and my lawyer excused themselves and held a private conversation in the far corner of the room. When they returned a

The New World Awaits

few minutes later, Mukamal winked at me and smiled reassuringly. The judge told me bail was set at $1,000. "I hope I *won't* see you again, young man," he said sternly. (Some time later, I heard that Steve's law firm had hired Judge Greenberg. I wondered if that might have influenced his leniency in my case.)

I called Kitty immediately, and she posted my bail within the hour. Drained and humbled, but free again, I went straight to Steve's office. He reassured me that Judge Greenberg had been sympathetic to my situation. I was now allowed to work both jobs, but he warned me not to leave the country again. He hoped to get my labor permit and Green Card within a few months now that I had a job offer from Kitty's firm. Sure enough, in July 1969, I got approval for my Green Card. I'd been in America less than a year, and now I could stay here safely!

6
A Life-Altering Encounter

May you travel in an awakened way,
Gathered wisely into your inner ground;
That you may not waste the invitations
Which wait along the way to transform you.
—JOHN O'DONOHUE

𝒢etting my Green Card was a game-changer. In October of 1969, I was (now legally) working two full-time jobs—at what was then the Central Park Sheraton, and at the Wellington Hotel across the street, at Seventh Avenue and 55th Street. I had also earned a management certificate from the American Hotel Management Association. I still felt unsure about a long-term career in the hotel business, even though that was the direction my career was taking. Perhaps it was not a coincidence that I was working at the Wellington, where many theater people stayed.

One morning around 8 a.m., after a long night shift at the Wellington's front desk, I was telling a racy joke to a female colleague from Switzerland with whom I had become friendly. Suddenly, a flamboyantly dressed man in his sixties cut me off mid-sentence.

"You shouldn't tell a lady that sort of joke in public!" he scolded in a heavy accent. I ignored him and continued my joke in German.

"That's not appropriate!" he reprimanded.

Annoyed and slightly surprised that he had understood me, I switched to French.

He interrupted again. "Do you speak Russian, too?"

"*Da, konechno,*" I answered in Russian. "Of course."

"Now, may I finish my joke?"

He ignored my request. "What other languages do you speak?"

"Hungarian, Romanian, and Hebrew," I told him. "Please let me finish my joke!"

I don't recall whether I finished the joke, but I do remember being shocked when the man—who introduced himself as Simon Semenoff (1908-1987)—asked me to come work for his company. He told me he was the artistic advisor for dance for Sol Hurok, which he explained was a major agency that managed and promoted famous musicians, conductors, orchestras, ballet and dance companies.[1]

I couldn't understand why this unusual man with the silk scarf and the elaborate coiffure would offer me a job less than five minutes after meeting me. Did he have a hidden motive? Probably. But he piqued my interest, and because Kitty had become my role model, I took a risk. We arranged to meet at his apartment on 55th Street near City Center a few days later. I asked Ellen to come along to offer a second opinion.

When we walked in, I was overwhelmed by the lavish décor. I was used to Israel, where blank walls and basic furnishings were the norm, and I had never encountered anything like the scene that now met my eyes. Semenoff's walls were painted deep, rich colors, and almost every inch of them was covered in paintings and photographs. Heavy silk curtains framed the windows, velvet and brocade was everywhere, and memorabilia adorned every surface. It looked more like a Matisse painting or a Nijinsky set than a real home. Semenoff was cordial and welcoming. It was clear that he sensed my discomfort and was trying to put me at ease.

A Life-Altering Encounter

"I understand that you spent some time in Israel," he said. "I'm looking forward to moving there . . ."

So, it turned out Semenoff *did* have an ulterior motive, though nothing as sinister as I had feared. He was planning to retire soon and relocate to Israel. He hoped that if he introduced me to Sol Hurok, I would give him some contacts in Israel, where he could survive on his meager American Social Security pension.

Born in Latvia as Simanis Shapiro, he was a character dancer with the Ballets Russes de Monte Carlo. Hurok brought Ballets Russe to the U.S. in the 1940s and encouraged Semenoff to change his name. The ballet disbanded eventually, and like most other members of the corps, he remained in the States after World War II. Semenoff learned English and started working for Hurok, who contributed significantly to the development and appreciation of ballet in the United States. As I got to know him, he told me his entire life story, including the tragic tale of how his wife, the mother of his three children, had abandoned him—"*un danseur noble*"—to run off with "a lowly Irish policeman." Semenoff was as melodramatic as he was flamboyant.

After telling me about himself, we chatted about Israel for a few minutes, and then he explained the job offer. "There's an opportunity for a tour manager with Igor Moiseyev," he said. "You speak Russian, so I thought you would be terrific." I had no idea who Moiseyev was (he led a major Russian-folklore group), but I didn't tell him so. I just listened attentively. The field of arts management was so foreign to me that I had trouble grasping exactly what kind of job Semenoff was offering. When he asked if I had any questions, I wasn't even sure what to ask. I thanked him for his time, and we left, wondering if I had made a decent impression but not taking the interview very seriously. A few days later, Semenoff took me to the Hurok office at 720 Fifth Avenue. Still, I wasn't surprised when he called to say that the Moiseyev tour had been postponed and that there was no position for me after all. "I'll call you when something opens up," Semenoff promised.

I assumed that would be the end of it. So I was quite surprised when the Hurok office called me a short time later to interview for the job of tour manager for Andrés Segovia (1893–1987). I met with Walter Prude (1910–1988) in November of 1969. He was an elegant, mild-mannered gentleman and Sol Hurok's vice president. (He was also married to dancer-choreographer Agnes de Mille.)[2]

He explained that my job would entail accompanying Maestro Segovia on his North American tours, some 10 weeks, January through March every year.[3]

As usual, Maestro Segovia arrived in New York at the beginning of January. We met in his suite at the Westbury Hotel on Madison Avenue. As I walked through the hotel's elaborate, formal entrance and approached the front desk, I felt anxious but buoyed by the idea that I was on the other side of the desk—not a hotel employee but a guest of the Maestro himself.

Segovia was a portly, gray-haired gentleman with black-rimmed glasses and a carved walking stick with a silver head. He was quite cool with me and clearly disappointed that his previous tour manager had left him. In retrospect, he was probably hesitant to commit to a new person—especially to a twenty-four-year-old who didn't speak Spanish. Although he spoke English, it was an effort for him. It seemed apparent the language barrier would be a non-starter, ironic for someone as multilingual as I was. We spoke some French, but the Maestro soon reverted to English. I wasn't sure what that meant.

I struggled to engage him and sat through a seemingly endless series of questions and puzzling comments from him in French and English. At last, he offered his approval.

My first assignment was to pick him up two days later at 6 p.m. for his concert at Lincoln Center's Philharmonic Hall. I arrived promptly at the appointed time, but he wasn't in the lobby. To my alarm, the front-desk staff told me the Maestro had already left. I rushed to Lincoln Center in a panic, convinced that this was the end of my impressive new job. I hurried through the back door and raced to his dressing room.

A Life-Altering Encounter

"Why were you late?" he demanded, catching sight of me.

I apologized profusely even though I hadn't been late at all. We both realized he had confused the time. He didn't apologize but suggested I take a seat while he continued to practice. We still had an hour until curtain.

Before meeting the Maestro I was not familiar with guitar music. After the first few concerts I started appreciating this wonderful new sound and before each recital after administrative duties I would sit mesmerized listening to him conscientiously practicing in his dressing room. I had the privilege of some 200 private mini recitals!

This rocky start was nonetheless the beginning of a twelve-year relationship. I took a three-month leave of absence from my hotel jobs in the winter of 1970, but after a second leave, they refused to take me back, so I found a job working nights at the Waldorf Astoria.

During my first few years as Segovia's tour manager, whenever we arrived in a new city, I would check the Maestro into his five-star hotel and then find small, inexpensive lodgings nearby for myself. When we were in LA, my regular spot was the Westwood Inn, which charged $7 a night but was lovely and clean. It was near UCLA, which meant the area was full of students and, therefore, cheap restaurants.

For the first few years, we ate most of our meals separately. But gradually, as Segovia stopped fearing that I would abandon him, he began to warm up. One night, he asked, "My dear, what are you doing tonight? Would you like to join me for dinner?"

"Of course, Maestro," I responded, honored by the invitation. "What time?"

Soon he encouraged me to dine with him regularly and insisted that I stay in the same hotel. He also invited me to accompany him to interesting social events.

On average, he gave two concerts a week. After each one, we ate together if we didn't have a social engagement. On one occasion, I decided to surprise him, and, upon returning from the men's room, I paid the bill.

"No, my dear. No!" he said when he found out. His tone was so firm that I realized I had overstepped my bounds. In retrospect, I think he didn't want me to be an equal. Our relationship was based on the understanding that I was to be his "son."

Segovia's tours usually included concerts in twenty to twenty-five major North American cities and concert halls, and they were always sold out. *Always.* Although he was then in his seventies and eighties, Maestro Segovia was on top of his game. His loyal fans across the country expected yearly recitals from their idol—and attended them religiously. I learned to protect him from crowds of well-wishers after each concert. Only a select few were welcomed into the green room.

The Maestro had a lot of friends and students in California, all fans of classical guitar. Among those I met and befriended were Michael Lorimer, a distinguished student of Segovia and a master guitarist himself, and Daniel Heifetz, a fine concert violinist. Both moved to New York, and, some fifty years later, Michael and I are still close friends. Segovia's legacy and the adventures we both shared with him are an important part of our friendship.

When we had days off during the California leg of our tours, I took side trips to exciting new places like Mexico City and Hawaii, with the Maestro's permission, of course. Among the many remarkable venues I remember with Segovia were Chicago's Orchestra Hall, Jones Hall in Houston, the Academy of Music in Philadelphia, The Dorothy Chandler Pavilion in LA, and Toronto's Massey Hall.

After Segovia's concerts and extended green-room receptions, we would sit down to a four-course meal, which always included a cheese course (his favorite was gruyere) and a rich chocolate dessert. I enjoyed this immensely because I had grown up loving elaborate desserts, especially the sixteen-layer *dobosh torte* with caramelized sugar on top cut with a red hot knife that was one of my mother's specialties. I didn't realize until many meals later that a dessert as visually and gastronomically spectacular as my mother's was a rare find. Looking back, I'm certain this was not a

A Life-Altering Encounter

Proustian Madeleine reverie but an exceptional talent on her part. Years later, the *dobosh torte* became a family staple for holidays in America.

We always ordered big steaks and baked potatoes, and the steaks were even bigger because the staff always wanted to please Segovia. I remember an elegant meal with Segovia at the Beverly Wilshire hotel on a terrace overlooking Rodeo Drive, with the attentive staff making every effort to meet our desires, and tasting my first king crab legs at a special dinner with the Maestro at a private home in Detroit.

Although I was pleased to be touring with Segovia, in the first few years, I often felt lonely and sidelined when among his friends and admirers. After a few years as his travel companion, however, our relationship deepened, and I found myself not only welcomed by his friends but making friends with them myself. Year by year, I started feeling more comfortable in this new way of life. I also delighted in learning the cultural subtleties that defined each city we visited, from Boston to San Francisco. Being young made it easier for me to adapt to American customs and manners than it was for Segovia, who was very set in his ways. He could be egotistical and narrow-minded, often ignoring artists whose talents didn't interest him. Although well-traveled, as a result, Segovia led a cocooned existence, even on the road. After we had toured together many years, he became freer with his judgments and opinions.

"I am a musician," Segovia would tell me. He believed deeply in the class structure that put kings and noblemen above regular folk, and, paradoxically, he derived his sense of importance from their approval. Announcing himself as a musician and nothing more was also his way of disconnecting from worldly or political concerns, rejecting any sense of responsibility for others or their plights, even at the hands of his own government. Pablo Picasso and others left Spain as a statement against the Franco regime, but not Segovia. He would never have risked compromising his place among Spain's elite. In those days, Spanish society was extremely hierarchical, and, though the bourgeoisie were always aspiring to the ranks of the aristocrats, lineage was usually critical for acceptance in "the proper circles." The upper echelons made an exception for Segovia, even though he came from a middle-class family, because of his talent and his fame. Eventually, I realized that his ego covered deep insecurity, a vulnerability that explained his need to be treated with respect by anyone he believed to be in a powerful position.

By 1972, after touring with Segovia for three years, I was starting to feel assured of my own security and more confident that the U.S. was really a stable democracy. I was on the road with Segovia when I learned of an event that almost shattered this confidence. A bomb had exploded inside the Hurok office and had killed Iris Kone, a young receptionist with whom I'd been friendly. The bomb was the work of terrorists who were targeting both the Hurok office and Concert Artists Management Inc. (CAMI). Hurok was injured in the blast, though, because someone thought quickly and smashed the glass in his office to provide fresh air, Hurok did not succum from smoke inhalation. The fire department carried him out. The right-wing Jewish Defense League claimed responsibility for the attack, citing Hurok's business partnership with the Russian government and his resulting importation of Russia's great performing artists during those years. At that time, though Israel was offering citizenship to all Jews, Russia refused to allow them to emigrate. "Let my people go," was the Jewish Defense League's slogan.[4]

I was shocked that this kind of thing could happen in America, and perhaps even more surprised that it was carried out by a Jewish organization. It evidently didn't occur to them that this partnership might open the door to communication and negotiation with Russia, nor that violence was never an acceptable means of political expression. After the attack, the office could not function for several days. I felt uncomfortable raising the topic with Segovia. I did not know how he felt about Jews, although perhaps I suspected that his elitism might extend to anti-Semitism. I also very much wished I were in town to attend Iris's funeral, as she had been one of only a few friends I had made at the Hurok office.

A Life-Altering Encounter

During the months I wasn't touring with Segovia, I sometimes worked as an assistant to John Wilson, the Hurok administrator overseeing performances at the Metropolitan Opera House. The job provided many colorful experiences. In the summer of 1971, Sol Hurok brought the Royal Ballet, starring Rudolf Nureyev and Margot Fonteyn, to the Met.[5]

I was in my office, just below orchestra level, completing some paperwork between the afternoon and evening performances, when Nureyev, thirty-three, stormed in with his assistant, Wally, in tow.

"I am *not* dancing tonight," he announced.

"What happened, Rudy?" I asked.

"My masseur didn't come. I will not dance!"

"Rudy, Mr. Hurok will kill us both!"

It was a hot summer weekend, long before the era of cell phones, Google searches, or even answering machines. Not surprisingly, I had no luck finding a masseur. When I broke the news to him, Rudy looked at me mischievously. "What about you?" he asked. A few minutes later, Wally, his sidekick, returned to my office, carrying the massage table. Although uncomfortable and obviously unqualified for the task, I agreed to try.

Wally set up the table and Rudy, wearing only briefs, hopped on and lay face down. His back muscles were overly developed from lifting and carrying ballerinas around, and the only experience I'd had with massage was working the knots out of my own muscles after playing basketball. Still, what choice did I have? I started to massage his back. After a few minutes, Rudy asked Wally to go get a sandwich. I immediately objected. Rudy had a reputation for trying to seduce anyone who crossed his path, and I was already in a vulnerable position. "If anyone leaves this room, it's going to be me!" I told them. Rudolf grinned and muttered something in Russian before putting his head back down so I could continue. When I told the story to a talented actor friend of mine, he responded, "I would have obliged!"

The massage lasted some forty-five minutes, with five-minute breaks to relieve the pain in my hands. Finally, King Rudolf declared that he was prepared to claim the stage. He seemed to think he had given me a gift by letting me massage him, but I had muscle pain for days. I hadn't exerted myself that much since my days of manual labor on the kibbutz in Israel. On the bright side, he gave me an autographed photo of him with Margot Fonteyn before he left.

Capitalizing on Nureyev's fame, Hurok organized tours titled "Nureyev and Friends" in 1972 and 1973, and appointed me the tour manager. The performances typically featured six dancers doing pas de deux. The *pièce de résistance* was "The Moor's Pavane," Jose's Limon's towering achievement and signature piece. Rudolf was sometimes joined by his partner Erik Bruhn (1928–1986).

Both my job at the Met and my time working for and traveling with Segovia allowed me to learn some of the intricacies of protocol, organization, union contracts, the handling of divas, and marketing, which was more complex than one would think. I began to wonder if I could stage my own productions. Perhaps I could find an unexplored niche. Sol Hurok had imported wonderful performing-arts groups, but he had not *exported*, and there was such richness in American performing arts. Why not take it abroad? I knew from bitter experience how few cultural offerings there were in parts of Europe. Aside from the operas my grandmother took me to, we had no access to live performances when I was a child, despite loving and listening to music all the time. Exporting American performances would also allow me to express my loyalty to my new home country. I had no formalized plan, no money, no backing, and most critically, no contacts, but I started to dream, all the same.

Hurok had been the first person to rent the Metropolitan Opera in the summer and to bring major ballet companies there, such as the Royal Ballet, the Paris Opera Ballet, and the National Ballet of Canada, starring Rudolf Nureyev (1938–1993) and Margot Fonteyn (1919–1991). The performances generated tremendous excitement, were almost always sold out, and introduced a number of renowned foreign artists to the American public. In addition to Nureyev, Hurok's clientele included such fabled

A Life-Altering Encounter

names as Arthur Rubinstein, Isaac Stern, Itzhak Perlman, and, of course, Segovia. Hurok was a formidable force in the performing-arts world, though unsurprisingly, I had never heard of him before I was hired in 1969.

Semenoff did, indeed, move to Israel on his sixty-fifth birthday. I think he would have been gratified that, in 1987, almost two decades after our first meeting, I brought the revived Monte Carlo Ballet to the United States for the first time since the 1940s, when he was a member of the company. He passed away just a few months before their U.S. tour, at the age of seventy-nine, in Texas. My cousin, a Viennese filmmaker named Robert Dornhelm had produced a documentary called *Children of Theater Street* in the 1970s, with Grace Kelly's support. When he heard that I was bringing the Monte Carlo ballet to the States, he offered to shoot a promo for the tour as an homage to his friend Grace.

7

The Birth of Living Arts

*M*y years at the Hurok office (1970–1974) taught me a lot about how to launch a production and a performing-arts tour. The more I thought about it, the more confident I felt about trying it on my own. Maestro Segovia had taught me how much artists distrust their agents, promoters, and producers, and I had learned much about the art of personal diplomacy on the job.

For example, I knew that artists generally consider managers, impresarios, and producers a necessary evil. My analyst wife likens them to stern parents: they set rules, keep performers in line, and can be taskmasters when necessary. But they also support artists' performances and love them for their talents. When artists are starting out, they're elated to have representation because it's the best road to exposure and professional success. Agents can arrange package bookings, pairing up newcomers with older, more established artists. ("You can have Isaac Stern if you'll take a talented unknown who needs the exposure. . . .") But after they gain fame and public acceptance, they tend to grow resentful of their "parents." Sometimes they accuse them of depriving them of earnings. Admittedly, there are unscrupulous agents who charge unwarranted monthly fees in addition to their commission. But managers also provide a vital service for performers by handling the business side of their careers, as I learned in the Hurok office. It's easy for performers to forget that agents and promoters have a business to run, employees to pay, expenses, overhead—and that they need to make a profit.

Ever since I'd arrived in the States in 1968, I had been fascinated by the dynamic cultural scene here and amazed at how receptive American audiences were to such a wide variety of performances. Although, ultimately, I hoped to export American talent, I knew more about importing performing arts, so it seemed a logical place to start. I decided to start by exploring some of the edgy summer festivals outside of the U.S. In August of 1973, I went to the Edinburgh Festival at the suggestion of my dear friends Shosh and Moti Cohen. I saw a one-act, one-man show called *Dreyfus on Devil's Island*, starring David Mouchtar-Samorai, an Israeli actor of Iraqi descent who had studied theater in England. The play—by Michael Almaz, an Israeli radio and TV personality who lived in London— is about the tragic true story of Alfred Dreyfus. A captain in the French army, Dreyfus was imprisoned on trumped-up charges in the anti-Semitic environment of Paris in the 1890s. The "Dreyfus Affair" became such a charged issue that it divided the French until Dreyfus was given another trial and acquitted in 1906, after more than 10 years of imprisonment. Needless to say, the story resonated deeply for me because of my own saga of injustice growing up, and I found it utterly compelling. I identified with Dreyfus and admired his perseverance and determination.

What's more, the show was tourable. All the props and costumes could fit into a medium-sized suitcase. *Dreyfus on Devil's Island* seemed ideal for my first production.

As soon as I got back to New York, I began canvassing theaters throughout the U.S. To my delight, I found that many were interested in presenting *Dreyfus*. That gave me the confidence to launch my first U.S. tour. In 1973, I launched my business, Living Arts, with two plays,

The Birth of Living Arts

Dreyfus on Devil's Island and *Monsieur Artaud*, about the life and work of Antonin Artaud. Artaud was one of the protagonists of The Living Theatre movement, which my then-friend-and-colleague John Gingrich suggested would make a perfect name for my new company. Living Arts, Inc. was born in October of 1973, and began its first tour in March of 1974 with *Dreyfus* and *Monsieur Artaud*. I was the producer, promoter, travel agent, and manager all in one. Almost fifty years later, I still recall some of the stops on the tour, even the obscure ones like St. Olaf College in Minnesota, just south of the Twin Cities.

Sadly, Sol Hurok died suddenly in March 1974 at age eighty-five. He worked passionately until his last days. The crowd of more than 2600 at Carnegie Hall overflowed with prominent artists and fond mourners. At age twenty-eight, I was just beginning to grasp the depth of Hurok's accomplishments and his power in the world of performing arts.[1]

Sitting at the funeral, I reflected upon how much I had absorbed working backstage at the Met and in the office, grappling with the threads of production that created the fabric of the magical opening nights. I'd learned about protocols, contracts, managing divas, negotiating with unions, and marketing. Because of Hurok's vision, I had begun on a very specific life path. He was such a presence. Here I was now, on the verge of my first undertaking, and he was gone. I had hoped to have more direct contact with him as I matured.

I kicked off the tour a few weeks later with four performances at The Kaye Playhouse at Hunter College in Manhattan, for which I was paid $3,200. "Wow!" The Kaye Playhouse is across the street from 700 Park Avenue, where Sol Hurok lived. Did this have any special meaning? Perhaps only to me. With Hurok's support, *The New York Times*' theater critic, Clive Barnes, had agreed to attend opening night.

Unfortunately, our first performance was plagued with acoustic issues. David didn't enunciate or project clearly enough for his voice to carry in a 700-seat theater. (I had initially seen him perform in a 100-seat venue.) Compounding the problem was his Hebrew-Iraqi-British accent and that the performance was part of a subscription series, attended by an older audience. It wasn't long before I started to hear people whispering to each other, "What did he say, dear?" "I don't know. I can't hear him!" The show was an hour and fifteen minutes long, with no intermission, so there was no way to get word to David. Perhaps I had been presumptuous to ask Clive to attend. My creeping sense of self-doubt gave way to full-blown panic as I watched audience members begin to trickle toward the exit. Before long, a third of the audience had left! Mercifully, Clive was nice enough *not* to review the show, but I remained mortified.

The next morning, I met David and Michael Almaz, the director, for breakfast, though none of us had much of an appetite. Fortunately, he realized he needed to project more and try to overcome his accent. We resolved the acoustic problems, and the show toured several weeks in the U.S. It was actually well-received, and I learned a lot. First and foremost: Never open in New York!

Though the tour only netted about $500, I felt encouraged enough to repeat the *Dreyfus* tour, which had been better received than *Monsieur Artaud*. Unfortunately, I lost money on the second tour—and learned another important lesson of show-biz producing. It's very difficult to gauge the cost and budget of a show before opening night, and therefore, to predict how successful it will be.

In the fall of 1973, after returning from the Edinburg festival I got an unexpected call from a stranger named Gene Robins. He explained that he had gotten my name from Emily Russo, a girl I'd been seeing after Ellen and I had finally parted ways. "Emily suggested I call you because you're in show business," he told me. Gene worked on Madison Avenue, lived in Scarsdale, and played tennis at the Masters School, which was then an elite girls' school in Dobbs Ferry, New York. (It's still elite, but now co-ed.) He explained that a fire had burned the school's theater down, but a state-of-the-art replacement had just been completed, and the school was enthusiastic about the idea of hosting a festival to introduce the new space to the community. Gene and I partnered to

The Birth of Living Arts

create the "Masters Festival for the Performing Arts," which ran in July and August of 1974, for six weeks. The school gave us the theater at no charge, and I managed to get funding from the New York State Council for the Arts, which allowed me to arrange for the Metropolitan Opera to perform *Madama Butterfly* at the Festival. I was also able to schedule an Israeli musical and the Rod Rodgers (1937–2002) Dance Company. Because these groups were generally well-funded, they were willing to participate in the festival with minimum remuneration. Gene and I managed not to lose any money, in fact we each earned $160, *and* we had a wonderful time. Despite a rocky start with Dreyfus, and the challenges of the Master's Festival, I was unstoppable, open to new opportunities in show business as precarious and unstable as it was.

The Hurok office continued for another two years, as Hurok had sold it to General Electric. But without Hurok himself, I was not sure what the future would hold for me. Nor was I prepared for the impact losing Hurok would have on the organization's ability to maintain their roster of notable musicians. Fortunately, although the office struggled for survival, Shelley Gold and Walter Prude gave me work as the tour manager for "I Solisti di Zagreb," and famous violinists Henryk Szeryng, and Nathan Milstein, in addition to "Nureyev and Friends."

In the summer of '75, I was working on a tour of Henryk Szeryng in the Hurok office now led by Sheldon Gold, after Hurok's death a year earlier. One day, a rather brash young man showed up, trying to communicate in German. The receptionist couldn't understand him, and someone suggested she call me. The man was wearing an out-of-date three-piece suit despite the August heat. His hair was greasy and his appearance disheveled. "Shpeek Gehrman?" he asked me.

"*Ja, sicher,*" I told him. But the moment he started speaking, I realized he knew little German, so I asked what his native language was.

"Hungarian," he told me.

I responded in Hungarian. Relieved to find someone who could understand him, he introduced himself as Zoltán Göröcs and launched into an explanation of why he had come to International Concert Management (ICM). I sensed there might be potential business here and suggested we go out for lunch. Göröcs devoured his meal as if he hadn't eaten for days, excitedly explaining between bites that he had a contact with a group called ATER (L'Associazione Teatrale dell'Emilia Romagna) in Modena, Italy, that promoted live music, dance, and theater throughout the country. ATER was dedicated to bringing performance arts to a variety of demographics, and they were now eager to import performing arts from the West, he said. I did in not know it at the time, but the Italian Communist Party in the mid '70s decided to shift their ideological orientation from an exclusive focus on Russia to a wider perspective including the West.[2]

I was skeptical about Göröcs, but nonetheless, we arranged for three of his contacts at ATER to come to New York in April of 1976, after my tour with Segovia ended, to see performances by several dance groups they might want to consider bringing to Italy. I showed them Pearl Lang and a few other small companies, but they were most enthusiastic about Ambakaila, the national folklore and Steel Band group of Trinidad and Tobago, whose mission was to promote Caribbean culture. I had seen them perform when Sol Hurok brought them to the U.S. in early 1974 and had been particularly taken by the charisma and talent of one of the acts—the Samaroo Brothers, a seven-member group that played popular music as well as classics by Mozart and Chopin on steel drums. I had kept Ambakaila's elaborate twenty-page brochure, hoping to call on them one day. This colorful vibrant multi-ethnic Caribbean troupe seemed perfect for an Italian audience.

I had practically no savings, but this opportunity had fallen in my lap, and I was determined not to let it slip away. I could understand most of the Italian my new friends spoke, but I was hardly able to hold a conversation with them. My initial exchanges were with Silvano Piovesan, an Italian musician who spoke German and who ran ATER, the cultural organization of the Italian Communist Party. The German

The Birth of Living Arts

I had learned during my short stay in that country years earlier proved indispensable in helping me navigate the early stages of the ATER relationship. And, to my delight, before the artistic advisor and administrators boarded their plane back to Italy, we had a signed contract for Living Arts to bring Ambakaila to the Spoleto Festival and on a tour in the summer of 1976.[3]

It was hard to believe!

I should note that, at the time, I had no understanding of how elitist European dance audiences were, or of the skepticism with which they viewed American performers. Dance and art from the U.S. had only recently made inroads in Europe—and with mixed results. In 1964, American artist Robert Rauschenberg had won the International Grand Prize, the Golden Lion, at the Venice Biennale[4], the art world's most coveted accolade, becoming the youngest and first American winner. French audiences were infuriated, horrified at the thought of the art world moving from Paris to New York, as a result.[5]

Even if Europeans were becoming more open-minded about American painters, they still weren't ready to embrace American dance on the continent. In 1964, Merce Cunningham got positive-enough responses from London audiences and critics to support a two and a half-week booking for Cunningham. But in Paris, they threw eggs and tomatoes at the dancers on stage.[6] Audiences in Cologne were still hostile when Cunningham toured again, eight years later. Even in 1982, Jacque Lang, the Minister of Culture, was whining that Americans were stealing the spotlight for creativity in the art world, performing arts, and otherwise.[6] Interestingly, this followed my major success presenting *West Side Story* in 1980–1981 at the preeminent Paris Théâtre du Châtelet.

To allay skepticism and build cultural bridges during the Cold War, the U.S. started exporting, among others, dance companies that showcased the American ballet aesthetic that the Russian-born George Balanchine was creating. His signature "neoclassical" style fused traditional ballet techniques with Broadway and Hollywood influences. It also emphasized speed, rhythm, and precision, and favored extreme extensions, turn-out, and athleticism, all to dizzying effect. Despite these efforts, the European mainland didn't warm up to contemporary repertoires by Balanchine-focused companies until the late '70s and early '80s. Even then, their enthusiasm didn't last. Countries soon formed their own small dance companies, and audiences favored them—a tendency reinforced by recession budgets and cultural nationalism.[7]

All this made ATER even more unique. Established by the municipalities of Emilia-Romagna in 1964, the organization's main goal was to showcase touring productions. The group became a model for collaborations among diverse entities in staging and touring national and international performing-arts groups, which was particularly noteworthy in view of its communist history. Until ATER came along, Italian audiences saw predominantly classical ballet. ATER was forward-thinking enough to sense a growing curiosity about American performing arts and to believe audiences would respond to something "new" from the U.S. It was a stroke of luck to meet them at this early-but-pivotal moment in my career, concurrent with the Commies' new openness to embrace western culture.

I was also lucky to be able to offer innovative dance companies substantial performance fees, courtesy of the Italian government, who wanted to endorse performing arts for the people. Looking back now, I realize what a unique time the 1970s were because the arts were so well-funded. Sadly, such valuable cultural offerings are no longer a priority for most governments.

8
So Much Depends Upon . . .

so much depends
upon
a red wheel
barrow
glazed with rain
water
beside the white
chickens.
—WILLIAM CARLOS WILLIAMS,
DOCTOR AND POET (1883–1963)

*I*f you've ever stood in the New Jersey Transit terminal of Penn Station in Manhattan, waiting for your track number to be announced, you might have noticed the poem "Red Wheelbarrow" inscribed on the wall opposite the automated ticketing machines. I love this poem. As a producer, I lean toward the black-and-white. Give me numbers, hard facts, a direct "yes" or "no." I think that's why this poem moves me. The verse is so hauntingly simple—no poetic flourishes or pretension. And yet there is a quality to it—perhaps the fact that it is so very everyday—that strikes at my core. "So much depends upon . . ." Well, everything.

William Carlos Williams was a doctor before he became a poet. I once read that his inspiration for the poem was a dying girl he treated in the hospital. As the story goes, Williams stooped at the girl's side to take her pulse and listen to her lungs. When he stood up, he looked out the window, and this is what he saw: the red wheelbarrow, the rainwater, the chickens.

It is this interpretation of the poem that moves me most. We don't know what the circumstances were. Perhaps the girl caught a cold that went untreated and turned into pneumonia. Or perhaps Williams looked out the window at the precise moment her heart stopped beating. We all have our red wheelbarrows—telephone calls, letters, missed connections. They are the moments in life that seem commonplace until something shifts in an instant, and suddenly the everyday becomes seismic. We recognize our wheelbarrows when we see them, but we never know when they'll appear.

Phyllis and I met at a New Year's Eve party on the Upper East Side in December of 1975. I knew immediately that she was unlike any other woman I had dated in New York. She was an exotic kind of bird, a self-proclaimed feminist who had taken part in the protests at Columbia in '68 and was now pursuing a PhD in psychology. She was sophisticated, intelligent, and intimidating. I'll never forget one of the first things she said to me.

"You know, Peter, I'm not sure you can handle an independent woman like me."

"Well," I retorted playfully, "we'll either have a very long or a very short relationship."

In our early courtship, Phyllis and I had no idea what to expect. I was European; she was a quintessentially modern New York woman immersed in the psychoanalytic community. On paper, there was not much to suggest compatibility, and yet we loved being together. Both of us were passionate about and deeply involved in our work. In the first few

So Much Depends Upon . . .

months of our relationship, Phyllis was seeing patients at her East Side apartment, and I was preparing to embark on Living Arts' first summer tour at Spoleto and beginning another ten-week tour with Segovia. Our mutual independence was, in some ways, what fueled our romance.

With some hesitation, I decided to invite Phyllis to the Segovia concert at Lincoln Center two weeks after we met. I was a little worried about what would happen when they met. How would Segovia, an old-fashioned man with plenty of sexist assumptions and my beautiful new girlfriend, Phyllis, an outspoken professional, react to one another? I had hoped to introduce them briefly at the Lincoln Center concert and then go on to the formal after-party without Phyllis, thinking that Segovia was best taken in small doses, at first. I knew she wasn't exactly thrilled by this suggestion, but she seemed serene throughout the concert. Afterward, a rush of people flooded the Maestro, and Phyllis and I were separated in the crowd. She decided to head home without being introduced, figuring it wasn't the right time. Meanwhile, I ushered Segovia onto the backstage freight elevator to get him to his limousine as quickly as possible. Who should be on that very elevator when we stepped in? An adorable woman who stared straight ahead as if she didn't know me. I worried silently that Phyllis was angry with me. Had I botched their meeting? We walked out to 65th Street—Segovia, his wife, and I getting into the limousine, and Phyllis hailing a cab after we left. While I fretted in the car with Segovia, Phyllis was regaling her cab driver with the sad and funny movie moment in which she noticeably ignored her boyfriend and his boss while trying to avoid an awkward moment. We've laughed about it all the years since. I'd worried about a possible combustion between the two, and instead, there'd been hapless silence. Ironically, it would be almost half a year before these two people, both central to my world, would meet, and when they did, it would be under remarkable and unforeseeable circumstances. When I returned from the Segovia tour in March, Phyllis and I continued our romance. I suggested she accompany me on a trip to Trinidad, where I needed to finalize the arrangements for my first international tour. Phyllis agreed to meet me after presenting a paper at the American Psychological Association in Miami.

My new partnership with ATER had brought me good fortune. I was traveling to a beautiful, sun-drenched destination to finalize Ambakaila's travel arrangements for the Spoleto Festival, a wonderful career opportunity for me. And at my side was my girlfriend, Phyllis Urman.

As soon as we landed, a dapper man wearing a three-piece suit and exuding Caribbean flamboyance greeted Phyllis and me on the tarmac at Port of Spain Airport. He introduced himself as Aubrey Adams. Educated in London, Aubrey (1919–2007) was an arts administrator in Trinidad and the driving force behind Ambakaila. He and I had been in regular contact about the Italian tour and my visit to Trinidad to finalize the program, but he brought unexpected news: the show needed a few more days of preparation before it would be ready for me to view.

"I've taken the liberty of arranging a little three-day hiatus for you two," Aubrey said. "There's a lovely hotel on the island of Tobago. All the logistics have been taken care of, so just go and get some R&R. We'll see you in a few days."

The next thing I knew, we were sipping Mai Tais by the pool at the upscale Mount Irvine Bay Resort, Phyllis enjoying a book while I conducted business in my swimming trunks, receiving phone calls from Europe and New York about the festival. Fax machines hadn't reached the Caribbean yet. When a phone call from Europe actually went through and a waiter seeking Mr. Klein called me to the bar to answer it, everyone took notice. It was great fun for someone who, only one year earlier, had been driving taxis and working odd jobs to make ends meet.

One afternoon in Tobago, I headed to the tennis courts hoping to play a set or two with a fellow guest. A pudgy, cheerful, middle-aged Black man in tennis whites was courtside, and offered to be my opponent. As the set progressed, so did our conversation, and I discovered that he was Dr. Cuthbert Joseph (1927–2011), the minister of culture of Trinidad and Tobago. After learning that I was taking Ambakaila on tour, he

So Much Depends Upon . . .

offered me fifty round-trip airfares between Port of Spain and London for the ensemble.

By the time Phyllis and I returned to Trinidad three days later, everything had fallen into place except that the program Aubrey was proposing was too long. I had learned from Mr. Hurok to always leave the audience wanting more. Once we agreed upon cuts, we finalized the program. Now it was time for more play.

I suggested to Phyllis that we visit my friend Jojo Naim in Caracas. When we arrived, Jojo flew us in his four-seater airplane, along with his toddler daughter to a tiny island with a minuscule runway, where we then boarded a catamaran to take us to an even *smaller* island for snorkeling. Jojo is a jovial character who enjoys creating the unexpected. He certainly succeeded with me. The whole experience felt unreal. Jojo and I are still close after all these years.

Phyllis flew back to New York a few days later, and I took a commuter flight to Aruba to visit my friend, Mike Groder. The festival in Spoleto was a mere four weeks away, the arrangements were set, and Phyllis and I had a wonderful vacation. I was thrilled that my trip to Trinidad had been so rewarding professionally and personally.

Mike and I hadn't seen each other in more than a year, and I was very happy to be reunited with him. He and I met in 1969, when I was working as a desk clerk at Wellington and he was a frequent guest at the hotel. We were about the same age, and we became instant friends. His father was a traveling salesman who had immigrated to Aruba from Poland to escape persecution by the Nazis; then, he settled down, married a local girl named Anna, and eventually opened The Panama Store, Aruba's first department store. A severe and demanding patriarch, Mr. Groder insisted that his three sons work for the family business. Mike was a buyer for the store, which explained his frequent business trips to New York. But he was a headstrong middle child with dreams of becoming something greater—perhaps a partner—in the family business one day, and he constantly struggled to stay in his father's good graces. In Mr. Groder's

75

eyes, Mike would always be an employee. A father-son partnership was out of the question. As a result, the two were always at odds.

Though he could never escape Mr. Groder's constricting expectations, Mike staged several acts of defiance, one of which was his purchase of a fifteen-year-old forest-green Toyota. This cranky lump of rusty parts was a foil to the family cruisers his father drove: hefty Cadillac convertibles with shiny chrome wheels and trunks that were easily the size of the bathroom in my apartment on East 81st Street. Buying that ramshackle secondhand car was one of many antagonistic gestures Mike directed at his father, but, in the end, it cost him dearly.

The night before I was scheduled to leave Aruba, Mike and I had dinner at a local restaurant by the beach, where a jazz pianist played the standards. Our conversation covered his resentment of his parents, but also lighter things, like our latest romances. Mike's spirits improved over dinner, and he flirted with a woman at the bar before the two of us left, cheerful in each other's company.

I remember the car ride home. It was late—around 2 or 2:30 in the morning—and we were laughing about some joke the waiter had made at dinner. Mike was at the wheel. The year was 1976: we weren't wearing seatbelts. Few people did in those days. (I'm not even sure his flimsy old Toyota had them.)

I remember approaching a dark intersection where we had the right of way. Suddenly, I saw a flash of bright flight in the periphery. I turned my head toward the driver's side window and in one terrible moment, perceived the light growing brighter as it sped toward us. Then everything went blank.

My memories of the moments after the impact are brief-but-slow snapshots in time, like thumbing through a flipbook in honey. I remember waking up in the ambulance on the way to the hospital, vaguely aware that something bad had happened. I couldn't move my head, and my forehead felt strange—not painful exactly, but a twinge of pressure, a dull ache. My right arm was pinned to my side under the gurney straps, but my left

So Much Depends Upon . . .

arm was free. I reached up to my forehead and shards of windshield glass came loose in my palm. Groggy and shaken, I tried to look to my left. I couldn't. As the ambulance sped bumpily toward the hospital, I reached out for Mike. When I touched him, there was no response. "Mike!" I called. "Mike?" Then we hit another pothole, and Mike's arm slipped limply from his gurney. I knew he was dead.

I must have blacked out again, because the next thing I remember is being wheeled down a bright hallway. I tried to focus, but my eyes wouldn't adjust. Fluorescent ceiling lights flew by in flashes as the emergency medical team rushed me to the radiography room. Flash one. Flash two. Flash three. I remember thinking, *Is this what it feels like to die?*

Five days later I awoke. I learned that Mike had been killed on impact and that the force with which my forehead had slammed into the windshield had shattered my C1 and C2 vertebrae. Known as the atlas and axis, these are the two most neurologically crucial vertebrae. It's worth noting that the injury I sustained was actually identical to Christopher Reeve's injury in 1995, when he fell from his horse. How I'd not only survived the accident but escaped immediate paralysis was a mystery to everyone who treated me. My nurse reported a conversation between the physician overseeing my case and the lab technician. The doctor thought the tech had given him the images from Mike's scan.

"You idiot," he fumed at the lab technician, throwing my X-rays in the garbage. "Give me the shots of the *living* guy, not the dead one!"

"I did," the technician replied.

"*This* is *not* the neck of a living man!" the doctor insisted, pulling the film from the trash can. "Or at least not of a man who will ever walk again."

Mike's car had hurtled into a house following the crash. As it turned out, the house belonged to a local doctor who was close with the Groder family. Jolted awake by the impact, he raced outside, witnessing the wreckage. Fearing a broken neck, the doctor took pains to keep my body as stationary as possible while in transit to the hospital. Later, when the radiologist studied my X-ray, he noted that the openings of my vertebrae—through which the spinal cord passes—were unusually large. Without this extra margin, my spine would most probably have been severed, consigning me to a wheelchair for the rest of my life. Because of a combination of initial onsite care and a fortuitous genetic quirk, I sustained no major lasting damage to my spinal cord. Still, about ten years after the accident, I began to feel inexplicably cold all the time. After several neurological tests, we discovered that my autonomic nervous system, located in the back of the neck, had, indeed, sustained damage. But judging against how much worse my fate might have been, this seemed a relatively small price to pay.

Later, I would realize that the car crash that had ended Mike's life and had nearly ended mine was my *red wheelbarrow*. So much of everything that happened after—the days, the months, the years—hinged on the events of that fateful night.

Despite the horrific ordeal I had just endured, I hadn't forgotten about work. It was urgent that I contact ATER immediately to confirm Ambakaila's attendance at Spoleto, but I didn't know a soul in Aruba. Who could I turn to for help? The Groders were aware of the accident and my serious condition, but perhaps understandably, they did not set foot in the hospital. More surprisingly, they offered me no assistance.

I thought of Phyllis. I didn't want to scare her off—she was recently divorced, and I had planned to move slowly with our new relationship. If I called her now, the gravity of my situation could catapult us into something much more serious than either of us had expected, or she would retreat—but it was a risk I would have to take.

When the nurse said I couldn't use the hospital's only phone, I refused to eat until she allowed me to make a call. From my hospital bed, which had to be rolled up to the telephone, I dialed Phyllis. Just the simple "Hello?" on the other end filled me with relief. Not wanting her to worry, I told her I'd had a "fender-bender" and that I'd be slightly delayed getting home. The painkillers must have persuaded me that I could pull this deception off, but looking back, their effect on my speech must have

So Much Depends Upon...

given me away. When Phyllis and I hung up, she immediately dialed the hospital and asked to speak to my doctor, who filled her in. Instantly, she made preparations to come and get me.

Phyllis became my lifeline. Thanks to her position at Albert Einstein Medical School, she was well connected. Most propitious was her friendship with Rita Ransohoff, a colleague married to the esteemed neurologist Dr. Joseph Ransohoff. Dr. Ransohoff had saved the life of White House Press Secretary James Brody after the 1981 Reagan assassination attempt. When Phyllis arrived in Aruba a few days later, she had all the arrangements in place for my transfer.

American Airlines had refused to transport me, but KLM had agreed. And so, on June 6, 1976, the hospital staff placed a makeshift neck brace made of metal pipes and leather on me. My Aruban physician accompanied Phyllis and me to our journey to New York University Medical Center. I was lifted directly onto the plane via a forklift normally used for loading meal trays and beverage carts onto the aircraft. Three window seats had been expertly removed in order to secure my gurney in the cabin. Though I was high on morphine, I vividly remember the plane filling with applause and hearty cheers when we finally landed at JFK. Little did everyone on-board know it was my first time entering the United States with an American passport. Not the quiet personal victory I'd expected upon my return, but a victory arguably more monumental, nonetheless. An ambulance greeted us on the tarmac and, once I had been forklifted out of the plane, drove me straight to NYU's University Medical Center. There, in a gesture I'll never forget, was my good friend, classical guitarist Michael Lorimer. Michael serenaded me with "Recuerdos de la Alhambra" by Francisco Tárrega, and "Asturias," by Isaac Albeniz. By this time, the morphine had worn off, and my wits were sharp enough to appreciate the moment.

The doctors decided not to operate but instead to construct a cast for my torso and chest that would support my head and neck, hoping that C1 and C2 would fuse naturally. The cast had Velcro closures, but I could remove it only when I was lying down. I left the hospital three weeks later and twenty-five pounds thinner, with a cast that made me look like a man from Mars. I have not seen anything like it since.

While I was in the hospital, Ambakaila was preparing to depart for Spoleto. I handled all the details of the tour from my bed in NYU Langone, reassuring the Italians that everything was in order. I hired a representative to manage the tour when the group arrived, but it was painful and disheartening not to be there. Still, I kept telling myself, *I should be thankful to be alive.*

Everyone, it seemed, shared that sentiment. In the weeks and months that followed the accident, people kept saying, "Someone was looking over you. How grateful you must be!" But after losing Mike, teetering on the edge of paralysis, and being forced to spend months in a straitjacket, my mood was more melancholy than joyful.

Just two months into my tenure as half-mummy, half-man with a body cast from my waist up, Phyllis and I decided to take a vacation to Europe. The Spoleto Festival was over, but I still wanted to get away and get back in the saddle. New York City and everything in it that summer had felt so stifling, so restrictive, that we both needed a reprieve and to refocus on work. And as for love, the accident catapulted our relationship to a new stage. We flew to Scotland, spent time at the Fringe Festival in Edinburgh, moved on to London, and then traveled south to Venice and the Mediterranean coast of Spain, where Segovia invited us to his villa overlooking the Mediterranean.

When he saw me in my cast, he hugged me gingerly and then looked me directly in the eye. Without a hint of pity or sarcasm, he said simply, "Fortune in misfortune." I didn't know if he meant surviving a horrific car crash or having Phyllis by my side. But he was right on both counts. That insightful comment was the greatest gift Segovia ever gave me. I have never been a quitter, but the accident had wrought in me an oppressive sense of defeat. I didn't know if I could bounce back. Segovia's sentiment gave me the courage to forge ahead.

So Much Depends Upon...

On a blustery December day, just six months after the accident, X-rays confirmed that my neck had healed. And, so, the cast came off at last. Phyllis and I were now living together, and, when I got home that evening, I found an envelope from my lawyer waiting in our mailbox. I tore it open and saw a check for $21,000—compensation for the damages and personal injury I had sustained in the accident in Aruba.

Though it sprang from tragedy, this little fortune changed the shape of things forever for me. It became the seed money for my burgeoning production company.

My joy continued to be tainted by sadness. You don't get over a loss as significant as the one I sustained that terrible night in Aruba; there is no closure after such a trauma. For years, I would awaken in the middle of the night drenched in a cold sweat, having re-lived some moment from the accident in my dreams. Mike's ghost still haunts me, though less than it once did. In the years that followed, I never forgot the words of Maestro Segovia: "Fortune in misfortune." When I needed it most, he gave me permission to beat on, a boat sometimes against the current, other times with it hoping for wind at my back but always keeping an oar at hand, just in case.

9
A Segovia Reprise

I learned a great deal from Segovia, both personally and professionally. Over the years, I became one of his confidants, hearing about his adventures with women and the reason he had to tour so much in his later life supporting his former wives and all his children, including his middle-son, who was a painter in Paris. I became closely connected with his New York intimates, such as Rose Augustine, who epitomized his formality and style.

Rose's much anticipated annual salon after Segovia's Lincoln Center performance was a theatrical tour de force in its own right. She held the event in her own townhouse, which was located on West Ninth Street, a typical West Greenwich Village street—a leafy block lined with townhouses from the early 20th century (Edward Albee had been its previous owner).

Rose (1930–2014) owned the factory that made the guitar strings Segovia used. One entered the house at street level and then climbed a narrow set of stairs to the second floor, which was elaborately decorated with 19th-century antiques, including large Black cherubs, offensive by today's standards, and a collection of guitars. It made a dramatic backdrop for formal cocktails and canapés served by white-gloved waiters. After this tantalizing opening act, we would climb another set of stairs for an elaborate buffet dinner. I have since been in many embassies and grand homes around the world, but Rose's townhouse remains the most vivid to me, whether because of my relative youth and inexperience when I saw it or because of the romance and panache of the parties I attended there, I don't know. Perhaps both.

The evenings at Rose Augustine's stretched into the early hours of the morning, with such guests as the consul of Spain, theatrical notables like Agnes de Mille, pianist Alicia de la Rocha, and various Spanish dignitaries. In February of 1977, still in a wheelchair after suffering a stroke in May of 1975, Agnes described how she had written a book, entitled *Where the Wings Grow*, from her hospital bed, barely able to move. Her amazing courage and creativity after such a debilitating blow to her body bolstered my confidence that I could also overcome any obstacles thrown in my path. I was still sorting through the shock and emotional scars from the car wreck, reflecting, of course, on my survival, after removing my brace a few months earlier.

I was always baffled by Segovia's insecurity, given his virtuosity and his fame. He always worried about being good enough. Presentation was of the utmost importance to him, and he had such strict protocol for clothing that being with him always felt like returning to the 19th century. Phyllis knew this when she dressed to meet Segovia on his terrace that memorable afternoon, and she dressed in a simple conservative frock. The next day, we ran into him as we left a restaurant. Phyllis was wearing jeans and a T-shirt, which was, of course, the typical style for young women in the 1970s. Segovia acknowledged our presence politely and continued on his way. I don't know if he noticed Phyllis's casual clothing or not, but she was mortified. As it turned out, Segovia's presentation did not fully reflect who he was: In the early 1920s, his first wife, while unpacking his suitcase after an extended South American tour, discovered nude photos of him with another woman. So much for Old World grace and decorum.

A Segovia Reprise

Despite his courtly manners, Segovia was woefully ignorant of the performing arts outside the classical music world—a fact that he sometimes had trouble hiding, even in front of the notables at green-room receptions and festivities he attended. In January of 1978, world-famous ballet star Natalia Makarova, whom I knew from my Hurok days, approached me before a Segovia concert. "I'd love to meet the Maestro!" she cried, embracing me in her warm way, as best she could at nine months pregnant. After the curtain dropped, I ushered her backstage. She extended her hand, and I made the introduction. It became clear that Segovia had no idea who Makarova was. Artists outside his area of expertise were rarely of interest to him. To his credit, he covered well and was as friendly as he knew how to be. As he aged, I often had to turn people away because his patience for meeting fans was limited.

Segovia's provincialism even extended to Agnes de Mille, who was married to his agent, Walter Prude. In March of 1978, Segovia felt obliged to attend a rehearsal of *Rodeo* at the Joffrey Ballet. The Maestro cajoled Phyllis and me into accompanying him. Agnes faithfully attended Segovia's yearly reception at Rose Augustine's. It would be inexcusable for him to refuse this invitation, especially after her stroke. When the Maestro walked into the rehearsal studio in his gentleman's suit and bow tie, the dancers stared in awe. Surreptitiously, I kept a close eye on him because we had just finished a substantial lunch at the Westbury, and I was afraid he would nod off. I sat next to him, just in case. He managed to stay awake, but I could tell he was relieved when the rehearsal ended.

Phyllis and I, on the other hand, were thrilled to see the Joffrey Ballet perform in such an intimate setting and touched to see Agnes back at work so soon after her stroke, making adjustments and corrections from her wheelchair. Little did I know that I would tour the Joffrey Ballet extensively just a few years later. I also later learned that Agnes' *Rodeo* was to become known as a quintessential "American" ballet supported by the State Department for international touring as an exuberant, free, and creative expression of American culture.[1]

And then there was Segovia's anti-Semitism. Of course, he knew I was Jewish and not only tolerated me but, in his way, even loved me. Still, his remarks about Jewish artists were common enough to chafe. His casual racism was tied not only to professional jealousy but to a strange combination of provincialism and his elitism, and because of it, I could not love him wholeheartedly. Ultimately, though, spending time with him taught me a valuable lesson in the complexity of human nature with its surprising contradictions.

In March of 1978, at Segovia's annual recital at the Kennedy Center in Washington, D.C., he was invited to a concert at the White House featuring virtuoso pianist Vladimir Horowitz. I was lucky enough to accompany him and chat with President Carter.

"You know, young man, I'm a great admirer of Maestro Segovia," President Carter told me. "I have all his records."

"Perhaps you'd be interested in organizing a concert at the White House for him," I suggested.

President Carter responded with enthusiasm and told me to call White House staffer Gretchen Poston to make arrangements.

The recital was to be held on March 11, 1979 and broadcast live nationwide on PBS.[2] By now, Segovia was treating me more like a friend than an employee, and he graciously offered me twenty tickets for the concert. I invited good friends as well as business contacts from Israel, Italy, Trinidad, and New York, knowing this would be an ideal opportunity to impress people who could help me with business.

Segovia had performed all over the world, but even for him, a nationally televised White House concert was a big event. His wife was elated and nervous which compounded Segovia's anxiety. The performance wasn't until 3 p.m., but we wanted to arrive early as we had been warned that the St. Patrick's Day parade would create traffic delays. I arranged for the White House to send a car to pick us up at the Watergate Hotel at 1 p.m. Phyllis and I piled in with Segovia, Emilita, and eight-year-old Carlos Andrés and arrived at the White House around 1:30. So far, so good.

A Segovia Reprise

Left: Peter, Fritz Mondale. Center Segovia, Carlos Andres, Emilita.

Segovia and Emilita were chatting happily with the Spanish Ambassador and the other guests. Everything seemed to be going flawlessly. Around 2:15, the Maestro glanced at his watch and announced, "I must practice!" I followed him to his dressing room, where he opened his guitar case and reached into his pocket for his glasses as usual. *"Madre de dios!"* he exclaimed, frantically tapping every pocket and realizing his glasses were nowhere to be found. He had left them at the Watergate—he *never* performed without them.

"Peter, please go to the hotel and get my glasses!" he said, a note of panic in his voice. In normal circumstances, the Watergate was an easy ten-minute ride, but at the moment, the roads were impossibly blocked because of the parade. There was no way I could go and get back in time for the concert. Trying to stay calm, I called the hotel manager. He hurried to Segovia's room, found the glasses, and managed to convince the local police to provide an escort for a messenger through the parade route to the White House.

The glasses arrived moments before the scheduled live-broadcast performance started, and we all heaved a sigh of relief. I was delighted to entertain my guests and my new business prospects at the White House. I couldn't quite believe it.

President Carter was at Camp David for peace negotiations between Israel and Egypt, the first peace treaty between Israel and an Arab Country. Vice President, Walter Mondale, officiated. The East Room had been decked with flowers and greenery.[2] The Spanish government presented Mondale with a sculpture of the Maestro's hands playing a guitar, titled *Homage to Segovia*, and then he introduced Segovia. Unfortunately, Mondale was so uneducated about the Maestro that he had trouble remembering his name.

In spite of all of this, the program was a great success. Several members of the Carter family were on hand, along with numerous dignitaries, to hear the eighty-six-year-old Segovia play. His forty-minute recital included music by Narvaez, Bach, Sor, Castelnuovo-Tedesco, Torroba, and Albéniz, much of which he had adapted and arranged, and concluded with a Catalonian folk song as an encore. Afterward, we celebrated with a reception and buffet supper at the White House.

The following spring, I went back on tour with Segovia. We were in Washington, DC, once again, when he told me that George Balanchine, artistic director of the New York City Ballet, had invited him to a ballet performance at the White House and that he would like me to accompany him.

The concert featured Baryshnikov and two principal dancers from the New York City Ballet, Heather Watts and Patricia McBride. The

A Segovia Reprise

more money touring with me, but it was no use. I had no choice but to leave him—and ICM. And, so, another chapter of my life came to an end.

Segovia's swan song continued, eight to nine weeks a year, for five more years as my Living Arts business thrived. We corresponded, and I attended his concerts faithfully whenever he came to New York, but when Phyllis and I saw him offstage, we couldn't help noticing that his attention span was diminishing. In 1987, Segovia woke up one morning in Madrid and announced to his wife he was going to die. He took an afternoon nap, and never woke up. A lengthy *New York Times* obituary remembered him as "one of the paramount concert artists of the century . . . a pivotal figure whose crusade on behalf of classical music left an imprint on musical history." His death marked the close of an important era in music, and in my life. His significance to me would always endure.

10
The Spoleto Years
(1976–1992)

During the 1970s and '80s, there were two major festivals—Nervi and Spoleto—that shaped summer touring in Italy. Everything they imported had to be *in prima nazionale*—a national premiere. In other words, no one in Italy could ever have presented it before. This guaranteed national press for opening night. After the highly anticipated *prima nazionale*, you were free to tour the company in question almost anywhere in Italy, generally on two-week or three-week tours following their Nervi or Spoleto premieres.

After the grand success of ABT and Baryshnikov at the 1977 Nervi Festival in Genoa, I became ATER's primary source of dance and musical theater imports from the Western Hemisphere. Italian opera houses, from La Scala to the small theaters, had a fall season for opera, a spring season for concerts and ballet, and a summer season they needed to fill with shows for subscribers. In those days, the opera houses had big budgets—and they had to spend the full amount they had been allocated, or their budget would be cut the following year. I would propose various performing-arts groups for the following summer, and administrators of the major Italian opera houses, including La Scala, would come to visit New York to see them. Among them was Carlo Maria Badini, (1925–2007), the administrator of La Scala. The resonance of La Scala had continued to echo for me from childhood to my pilgrimage to Milan. Badini, along with Gian Carlo Menotti (1911–2007), founder of the Spoleto festival and a prolific composer (*Amahl and the Night Visitors*, *Antony and Cleopatra*), would travel to New York for me to showcase the next summer's offerings.

Few of the visiting opera-house administrators spoke English, so I was forced to draw upon my Romanian roots and learn *Italiano presto, presto*. I was pleased by how enthralled my Italian visitors were with New York, and how enthusiastic they were about the diversity and richness of the contemporary dance I showed them. At the time, I didn't realize the historical significance of these trips. I knew that Europeans were enamored with American pop music and blue jeans, but I thought most of the bourgeoisie was still grounded in a classical sensibility. In the 1970s and 1980s, few Italians spoke English, and they considered American musicals a superficial art form.

Being European myself, I gained their trust and introduced my Italian associates to America's cutting-edge performing-arts groups, as well as many of our classical performers, and was rewarded with their enthusiasm. It was in this ambassadorship, in my talent for conveying jewels of American culture, in my understanding and transferring of American sensibility, that I began to really find my sense of self. I was growing past the dislocated young soul I had been, that young man wandering the streets of Italy at Christmas, overwhelmed by the cheer in the air. Under Communism, we'd lived under a menacing suppression of our autonomy, our individuality, our very souls, a subjugation to a faceless State. Aside from the lavish opera houses, maintained as a way to placate the otherwise culturally malnourished population, there was little joy to be found behind the Iron Curtain. Children, born with an

The Spoleto Years (1976-1992)

ability to experience a sense of self through personal expression, grew up incapacitated by the gloomy banality of this authoritarian universe, our emotional development stunted. Through Living Arts, I was at last able to express my personal gifts. My company was a rebirth, a chance to develop the soul starved in youth. Here was the promise captured in the pages of my grandfather's art books—the majestic doors of La Scala were now unlocked and flung wide open. My life was no longer about denial and longing, but about the thrill of pursuit and the joy of achievement. I thought of my parents—so forlorn and lost in Israel, struggling to build a life they had long dreamed of—and wondered if there was a point at which it was too late to rebuild. My parents had worked hard for my freedom and gotten me out before I'd calcified. This new life, this new identity, was not only mine, but my monument to their struggle. They'd kept our souls warm behind closed doors, with books and music and love, and then they had set us free in time for us to grow. American culture had given me nourishment, and my role as ambassador, as cultural catalyst, as budding impresario, allowed me to express my gratitude to my adopted country.

Even today, some of my aristocratic Italian friends will complain about the Ara Pacis Museum in Rome, or the new opera house in Florence, bemoaning modernity. I have learned that Americans generally embrace the new, while Italians often approach it with skepticism. After all, their identity is intertwined with their magnificent Renaissance past. (Interestingly, that tendency may be shifting. I notice that more Americans now seem to want to hold on to the past. Meanwhile, many Italian artists and designers are finding ways to integrate the new with the traditional.) Americans continue to make their mark in Renaissance Florence, as evidenced in the Levett collection, housed in a grand Palazzo on the Arno, with a significant collection of post-modern women American artists such as Elaine de Kooning and Louise Bourgeois.[1]

Despite the overall traditionalism in Italy, my contacts there were enthusiastic about exploring offbeat venues such as La MaMa

Experimental Theatre Club and Off-Broadway shows. In addition to arranging private performances of dance companies in their rehearsal studios, I developed a routine that captured the grandeur of New York from different perspectives. I would take my visitors to the top of the World Trade Center. They were mesmerized by the height of the building and the spectacular views of the Statue of Liberty and beyond. We would finish the evening at the River Café, which was nestled under the Brooklyn Bridge and offered a very different but no less intoxicating view of the skyline.

Many years later, I learned that that River Café was a Mafia hangout. I was dining there with a musician friend named Van Joyce, a talented composer, producer, and impresario himself. Van went to the men's room, and on his way back, he flirted with a woman at another table. Moments later, a burly man put his hands on Van's neck. The man was smiling, but I noticed that Van's face had begun to change color. The stranger was squeezing hard enough to inflict serious pain. Then, he hissed a warning in Van's ear and walked away. Shaken, Van and I paid the bill immediately and left. The restaurant's extensive and extravagantly priced wine list now made more sense.

Many of my Italian contacts were first-time visitors to New York, which made witnessing their experiences here both poignant and satisfying for me. Whether from taking in views or realizing the myth of New York City, their excitement was palpable. In those days, of course, the World Trade Center towers shone brightly at the tip of the skyline. How provincial Italy must have seemed to them by contrast with this futuristic, glittering monument to modernity, electric with vitality. Whenever I returned to Spoleto, the fast brightness of New York faded into the background for me, too. In Italy, traditionalist thinking was pervasive, but our American imports were changing the performing-arts landscape there, too. After all, my vocation was about forming ties among cultures, about knocking down borders, and about globalism. Only years later did I consider the imperialistic rhetoric

The Spoleto Years (1976-1992)

which may have been part of this effort, and which was at the time resisted by the Italians and others.

After ABT's success at Nervi and some other successful presentations in Spoleto, some of my Italian colleagues started calling me *"Il re della danza."* I was quite surprised by this and unsure that I could live up to the title. Nonetheless, it afforded me some wonderful perks, including an invitation to the home of a Roman *contessa* in the charming medieval village of Campello sul Clitunno. A friend of Menotti's, she had heard about my role in the festival.

Turning off the main road between Spoleto and Foligno, and driving along a narrow, unpaved driveway, Phyllis and I arrived in a different world. The countess's home, called *Il Mulino*, is in a historic grain mill, with beautiful ivy-covered stone buildings that exuded hundreds of years of tradition. A lovely little stream ran alongside it, and a veritable welcoming committee of ducks waddled up to greet us as we stepped out of the car. The estate also boasted a trout pond and an historic site dedicated to Dante Alighieri in the hill nearby, most likely built by Hugo, Duke of Spoleto, in the 14th century. Life in this quaint rural corner of Umbria seemed to have changed little over the centuries.

The *contessa* treated us with grand Italian hospitality, providing us with wonderful meals, often with fresh trout. Rural Umbria embraced the farm-to-table concept long before it became trendy, though of course, no one used the phrase in those days.

At Il Mulino, we awoke to birds singing and a beautifully set table on a little peninsula in the middle of a stream. We had fresh bread and cappuccino, often served with Italian *dolci* for breakfast.

On hot summer days, we retreated to the cool hills in search of remote trattorias, many of which specialized in *tartufo estivo* (summer truffles) and *stringozzi*, the long spaghetti-like pasta typical of Umbria. One of our favorites had a large toucan that welcomed each guest. The days were sweltering—much too hot for wine at lunch—but the nights were pleasant, with the melody of cicadas in the background, and we drank plenty of wine after dark. We tried with difficulty to restrict ourselves to a two-course lunch because, though performances often began as late as 9 p.m., I knew I had to be at the theater by 6 p.m. on opening nights. This left little time for a much-needed siesta. My cursory knowledge of Italian came in very handy on these trips, because as soon as you left the vicinity of Spoleto, you had to speak the local language. ("*No Inglese, per favore.*")

One evening when the countess was traveling, she suggested we host dinner at Il Mulino. We were pleased to invite the great American choreographer Glen Tetley (1926–2007) and his partner, ABT ballet master Scott Douglas (1926–1996). Glen regaled us with fascinating stories about Umbria as we gazed at the monument to Dante in the hill above us.

We revisited Il Mulino several times when I presented other attractions at the festival, and it earned a special spot in my heart. By that time, the countess had begun to offer the property as a guesthouse, with six or seven rooms available exclusively for people from the festival. Perhaps it was the sound of the gurgling brook, or the magnificent dinners prepared especially for us, but our first trip here will always be my fondest memory of the place. When we were the only guests in this enchanting, romantic spot; it was our own private discovery. Only a short ride from the crowds and excitement of the festival, it felt like a world away.

The Spoleto Years (1976–1992)

In 1979, I brought *Crowsnest* and the *Ballets Trocadero de Monte Carlo* to Spoleto. *Crowsnest* was a small, genuinely theatrical dance group founded by Felix Blaska, Robert Barnett, and Martha Clarke after leaving Pilobolus Dance Theater in 1978. *Crowsnest* opened at Caio Melisso, a boutique gem of an opera house built in 1668. Martha was an instant success, with her witticisms, drama, and lusty theatricality. I was prepared to take a chance on these edgy companies, although I was equally concerned about reviews, because my reputation partially hinged on them. I was also preoccupied with what new groups I could propose for the coming year. Happily, the two main Italian dance critics—Vittoria Ottolenghi (1924–2012) and Alberto Testa (1922–2019)—lauded the *Crowsnest* program as an engaging, eclectic new dance form.

Already a New York phenomenon, *Ballets Trocadero de Monte Carlo* was and remains a very technically accomplished all-male ensemble that gave audiences a good laugh with their parodies of the "Dying Swan" and the "Pas de Quatre" from *Swan Lake*. The Italians found their work innovative and refreshing.

Those summers were delightful, but interwoven with the excitement and artistic challenges of the performers was the uncomfortable reality of predictably late payments. I began to understand that it was easy for opera and festival administrators to commit to a tour, but if someone new won the next election, the administrators themselves would be replaced—and their replacements would decide how to allot their budgets for the arts. Most producers wouldn't have tolerated the arrangement, but my work in Italy helped me expand tours to other European countries and to Israel. I found it hard to close the door on the constant delight that was Italy. There was a sweetness to those years that has proved incomparable. Phyllis suspects some other motivation for my accepting the continuous financial instability of those contracts, perhaps some need to maintain my position and reputation, or else some quiet pain from childhood never fully resolved. In truth, I am certain it was simply the pleasure of Italy's embrace, the nourishment of their culture, land, and exquisite food. In all ways, we were well-fed in those summers, and accordingly, we blossomed.

As the years progressed, I established a significant presence in Italy as a New York impresario and became less dependent on launching my tours at Spoleto. My credibility gave me more room to take artistic risks and more confidence to advocate for avant-garde dance companies that I had discovered. Italian audiences and critics weren't always as open to contemporary and experimental groups as they professed to be in the 1980s, but Menotti was feeling increasing pressure from festival-goers who claimed Spoleto had become mundane and predictable. He was therefore more receptive to my riskier proposals.[2]

In 1983, we returned to Spoleto with one daughter in tow and another on the way. With help from the festival administrator, we had arranged lodging in a spectacular villa overlooking Spoleto. The Contessa who owned it needed money because her husband, Count Enrico Datti, had recently died of a heart attack in his early forties. I knew it was a grand villa, but I wasn't sure what to expect as we wound our way up through a beautiful old olive orchard in the Umbrian hillside, a short way from the famous Roman aqueduct. We entered through a large wrought-iron gate and were greeted by the *contessa* and her dog. Our daughter Nadia, almost three at the time, adored the dog. She learned *"vieni qua"* ("come here") very quickly. The countess showed us a rather intimidating straight staircase made of *pietra serena*, the gray stone common in Renaissance Architecture. There were six bedrooms and an *ironing* room. (I later learned that many Italian women are fanatical about ironing. To this day, you can visit electronics stores in Italy and find countless different kinds of irons.) During our stay, the contessa retreated to a small cottage on the grounds, though every morning she offered us a basket of eggs and fresh herbs from *il giardino di spezie*.

The villa provided the perfect opportunity to entertain colleagues from around the world. Taking a page from my days in the hotel business, I posted a schedule in the kitchen of who would be staying where

The Spoleto Years (1976–1992)

and when, to keep track of guests' arrival and departure dates and room assignments.

Phyllis suddenly found herself in the role of a grand dame living a 19th-century lifestyle, including feeling abandoned by her prince, who was thrilled with the opportunity to welcome all his international partners in grand style. Although she was the *donna di casa*, she was also pregnant, alone, and angry about being relegated to a traditional caretaking role.

Every morning, our guests gathered around the villa's large dining-room table to debate whether the festival had deteriorated under Menotti's administration and whether it had "strayed" from its original avant-garde, experimental mission in favor of commercial appeal.[2] Phyllis had little patience for these passionate diatribes and preferred to go into town to the *salumeria* to get supplies for lunch and breakfast the following day. I was left to engage the guests while tending to the inevitable complications of the performances. The dispute over the quality of the festival would continue through lunch, until our guests broke for a compulsory siesta. In the late afternoon, everyone would rise and dress for the evening of drama and dance, before returning to the villa for *grappa* and more animated discussion.

During this summer, we reconnected with Glen Tetley, who had restored an enchanting watchtower built into the hills of Spoleto and accessed by a dirt road that passed through the contessa's property. We enjoyed lunch with Glen and Scott on their terrace, and I remember being impressed by the bathroom, which was carved out of a rock.

Naturally, we invited Glen and Scott to the villa. We were sitting in the living room, enjoying the evening, when he told us that this was his first time in the grand house, because the Count had been homophobic and hostile to gay foreigners. In fact, he had refused to allow Glen and his partner, Scott, through the main gate, forcing them to take the back road through the chicken coops after a dramatic altercation. Glen and Scott had nicknamed this dirt road "Chicken Shit Hill."

THE LAST IMPRESARIO

A few nights later, while enjoying a *risotto ai funghi*, Glen regaled us with a story of Jerry Robbins that highlighted the extent of the count's animosity. He, Jerry, and twenty dancers had been on their way home from a performance in a caravan, circling up the mountain road to Glen and Scott's tower when they were confronted by Count Datti and several of his *amici* on horseback with torches returning from a nighttime hunt. The Old World aristocrat was furious that dancers, and particularly gay men, were "intruding" on his property while his wealth, status in society, and territoriality were being challenged. Jerry had the misfortune to be sitting in the passenger seat of the lead car. The count grabbed him by the lapels, dragged him out of the car, and threw him against the hood. *"Qui non si puo' passare!"* the count growled, which basically translated to, "You are not welcome here!"

Glen was terrified the confrontation would take a violent turn, but fortunately, after a few verbal threats, the men rode off into the night. Following that harrowing and embarrassing event, Glen took the Chicken Shit Hill detour to his watchtower *casa* gladly to avoid the Count. He refused to go near the villa until after the man's death.

In 1984, in response to the demand for edgier spectacles at Spoleto, I suggested Byakko Sha, a Japanese dance troupe whose work was inspired by the controversial Japanese surrealist dance movement known as Butoh. A German colleague whom I had met at Spoleto the previous season and respected a great deal had recommended the group highly, and Maestro Menotti was onboard immediately. Without hesitation, I went to Kyoto to see them on stage. I knew their work was unsettling, but they were also bold and talented.

The group's performance was called "Dancing in a Pool of Grey Grits." They began with very theatrical, exotic Asian music and movement, but after the first few minutes, the real spectacle unfolded. The performers hurled everything from bananas to pieces of broken watermelon and live chickens at the audience. Those in the first few rows hurriedly left their seats to stand in the back. "Outrageous!" and "Not acceptable!" were a few of the comments I heard.

The Spoleto Years (1976-1992)

Many people were scandalized by the production, and I was afraid I had unknowingly gone too far. Would this ruin the reputation I had worked so hard to build? But much to my surprise, the critics raved.

They had no idea that, backstage, the scene was appalling. When the group arrived, I was shocked to see their leader, Isamu Ohsuka, insulting and physically abusing the female dancers before and after the performance. I made it clear that this was unacceptable in the West, as I was quite eager to stop the abuse. Ohsuka responded in Japanese and became a bit more discreet, but sadly, I knew there would be little change in their behavior. I was afraid to approach the women, and my hands were tied anyway, since we didn't have a shared language.

I later learned that Byakko Sha's behavior was even more sinister at home in Japan. Ohsuka created what he called a "supportive" environment. In reality, it was a cult that violated basic human rights. The female dancers spent their days rehearsing the company's repertoire and their evenings working in the red-light district and bringing their earnings to Ohsuka. The women were effectively enslaved.

Later, when I befriended my main performing-arts contact in Japan, Takada, and visited him there, I was not surprised that it was pervasive in Japanese culture for women to attend to men in ways that were shocking to me. One weekend, he invited me to his country house, and, though his wife wasn't in attendance (he proudly stated that she never set foot in "his" leisure home), his niece catered to us like a servant. She was there solely to serve us. When I pointed out this inequality, he changed the subject. I didn't want to push him too hard since he was a friend as well as a business partner, but it highlighted the delicate diplomatic balance I had to strike in my work and the limits of our capacity to truly "enter" another culture.

In the summer of 1985, Phyllis and I hired a Columbia University student named Fatima to serve as an au pair for our two daughters, now one and a half and four and a half years old. Fatima was gentle and wonderful with the children, and we looked forward to having her join our family for a summer in Europe. She would accompany us to Spoleto, where we were planning to stay at a charming old farmhouse owned by an Argentine sculptor, and to France for a vacation afterwards. Big drama unfolded the evening before they were to leave New York for Rome, when Phyllis called to inform me that Fatima, a citizen of Nicaragua, had a Green Card only; she was not yet a citizen. She needed a visa to enter Italy. In those days, border control was much more *laissez faire*, especially if you had important political connections, so I hoped the Italian authorities would let her in if she were with us. I reassured Phyllis that I would handle it. "Just take the flight," I said. In the '80s, you could *leave* an American airport to go abroad without showing any form of identification. As incredible as it seems now, all you needed was a boarding card. United States authorities didn't generally check to see whether you would be able to actually enter your destination. In some ways, it was a more casual world than it is now. Often guards would be seen taking their siesta in the middle of their workday. Phyllis was worried, but she and Fatima agreed to take the risk based on my reassurances.

Unfortunately, when they arrived at Fiumicino in Rome, the Italian officials refused to let Fatima enter the country. I was allowed into the arrivals area to deal with the crisis but was assured that they were "*assolutamente*" sending her back on the next flight. I was shocked that they were so definitive about it, and Phyllis and I felt a bit overwhelmed at the thought of six weeks' vacation with no help. Furthermore, Fatima had planned her whole summer around this opportunity but was careless in not checking until she was ready to depart.

"You have to do something," Phyllis cried.

During my many trips through Fiumicino with my performing-arts groups, I observed that there were no passport controls from the *arrivals* section into the *departures* section, a shortcoming of Italian border control. Not a coincidence: I was painfully trained during my many years behind the Iron Curtain that there were no loopholes. There is a reason the "Curtain" was called "Iron."

Thinking quickly, I told Phyllis to leave the airport with Nadia and meet us outside Customs. Then I picked up Alexis in my arms and told

The Spoleto Years (1976–1992)

Fatima to follow me back to the departure area. There was only security control here—no documents necessary. Once in the departure area, acting casually, with the baby in my arms, I waved three passports at the guard, explaining in Italian that I was going back out because I'd forgotten something. Sure enough, the guard glanced up from his papers and waved us through with a lackadaisical, "*Vai, vai.*"

We reunited happily outside Italian customs and left Fiumicino together, speeding gleefully along the highway toward Spoleto, literally heading for the hills. I thought Menotti or his administration would be able to rectify the situation when we arrived. I didn't realize that the only way for Fatima to obtain a visa was to return to the U.S. Neither the American Embassy nor the Nicaraguan Consulate could help. It became clear that Fatima wouldn't be able to leave Italy legally.

As I write this, I am aware of the increased controls on borders, and I am humbled to reflect upon the ease with which people traveled in non-Communist Europe and most parts of the world post-WWII. Intense security and scrutiny were unknown, and no one dreamed of a suicide bomber boarding an airliner. Such freedom of movement was a stark contrast to my experience under Communism, of course. When I returned in 1980 with Phyllis and traveled by train from Timișoara to Budapest, border police were on the train looking for stowaways, just as they had been decades earlier.

When Spoleto ended, I faced another dilemma: How was I going to get Fatima to France, where we'd planned to spend August?

Ventimiglia, the border between Italy and France, had two checkpoints—one Italian, one French. Parallel to them was a building with banks and shops. On previous trips, this had repeatedly caught my eye, and it registered as an obvious loophole. I well remembered my Dad's advice: "Don't just look—*see!*" Authorities checked the passports of people in cars, but it was easy to simply walk in and out of the various Italian and French offices on the side of the passport-control booths and get across without anyone checking. In retrospect, it seems hard to believe how lax they were. No one else may have even taken notice, but my immediate association to ten-feet-high barbed-wire fences, along with elevated army posts guarding every possible exit from Romania made this informality all the more striking.

I assured Fatima that we would be able to walk through without a problem.

"Are you sure?" she asked. "The embassy said that I should be careful. I could be sent home."

"It will be fine," I said. I got out of the car with my adorable eighteen-month-old Alexis in my arms. "Just follow me."

Fatima followed the baby and me with trepidation, while Phyllis waited in the car on the Italian side of the checkpoint. Fatima and I went into the bank and changed some money. Then we walked from the Italian bank into a shop, trying to act nonchalant. Next, we strolled into the French bank to exchange more money. *Et voila*, we were in France. From the exit of the French bank, I signaled to Phyllis, who was anxiously waiting in the car. She drove across to France with Nadia, stopping to have their passports checked by both border authorities. I find it sadly ironic that it was easier to cross this European border in 1985 than it is in 2022, with the European Union confronting a migrant crisis.

That summer we stayed at a large estate in Lambesc, halfway between Aix and Avignon, which was owned by a Dutch family with a contemporary-art collection. We chose a large home because we had hoped Phyllis' parents and my family would join us, but, unfortunately, her father was suffering from pancreatic cancer, which had progressed to a stage that made him reluctant to travel.

The villa was ideally located for touring Provence. We had fresh vegetables from the garden and escargot prepared Provençal style in tomato and green pepper sauce by the housekeeper on the grounds. I also engaged in late-night discussions with a local doctor who spoke only French. He complained bitterly about the influx of immigrants to Marseille. We were shocked by his racism, as naïve as that sounds. Provence seemed a

The Spoleto Years (1976–1992)

peaceful paradise to us, but the world was changing fast. By 1985, France was already having trouble integrating the African migrants landing in nearby Marseille, and thefts were on the rise, especially in grand villas not far from the coast. We were in a gated property, and we were warned that the gate should be kept closed at all times.

The following year, while summering at Villa Gezanne in the village of Biot on the Côte d'Azur, we encountered a similar concern about robbery. We considered the large, imposing gates at the entrance part of the villa's charm, but in retrospect, we were ignoring the tensions simmering under the glamour of the Côte d'Azur. Our villa was tranquil and secluded, but at the markets in Cannes and Nice, the increasing presence of recent immigrants was obvious. The foundation of France's national identity was homogeneity, but by the 1980s, diversity was a growing reality.

In the late 1980s, budgets tightened, and Italian theater administrators no longer had the funds to support extravagant visits to New York. Forced to be much more frugal with expenses, they began to go directly to each source for festival engagements. At the same time, after fifteen years, my passion for the *Spoleto Festival* was dwindling. In 1992, I discovered the Robert Desrosiers Dance Company of Canada, a vibrant and innovative contemporary-dance troupe from Montreal that pushed traditional notions within a mixed repertoire. It seemed perfect for Spoleto, as I told Menotti, and he enthusiastically agreed to include the company, despite the cost.

A few months before the festival in 1992, I received an unexpected invitation to attend the opening night of the Festival delle Ville Vesuviane, an invitation-only event at Torre del Greco, south of Naples. I knew Rudolph Nureyev had been suffering from AIDS for some time, and I thought he had retired. Now I realized he was determined to dance until the end, and I was intrigued by the possibility of seeing him perform once more. This was a small, last-minute gathering for an exclusive performance with Nureyev—a special opportunity, since Ville Vesuviane was not far from Le Sirenuse, "King" Rudolf's private island. Our daughter, Alexis, had not yet begun overnight camp, so she joined us for the adventure.

Arriving in Naples and driving south, I noticed with unease the impoverishment of the neighborhoods we passed through once we got off the highway. We saw extensive graffiti and garbage, along with an occasional elaborate Disney-like hearse bearing religious figures and caskets.

"Are you sure this is the right village?" Phyllis asked.

After about thirty minutes, we arrived at a convent-like enclosure with massive walls and a large gate.

Inside the villa was a small stage and seating for about two hundred guests. Nureyev performed *L'Après-midi d'un faune*. The angular, stylized, slow-paced choreography was perfect for his ailing body. It was painful and touching to see. At some points, it seemed uncertain that he would be able to complete the performance, but he had four skilled and sensitive ballerinas who bolstered him during the more difficult parts. Although we didn't realize it at the time, this would be Nureyev's final performance. He retired to his island a short boat ride away and died a few months later, on January 6, 1993, in Paris. This final memory of Nureyev, engraved in my mind, serves also as a monument to the scope and breadth of the AIDS crisis in those years and the gruesome way in which it ravaged so many of our finest artists.

We left for Spoleto the day after the Nureyev performance, and after four hours of driving, arrived in time for my presentation of the Desrosiers Dance Company. Arts critic Vittoria Ottolenghi drove with us. Around 1990, Menotti hired Vittoria and Alberto Testa to select dance companies for the festival. Interestingly, these two were also the major dance critics in Italy, and Vittoria had a dance program on RAI. Neither she nor Alberto Testa nor Menotti himself saw the conflict of interest in writing a review about a company they themselves had selected.

After the performance, we were invited to a reception at the American consul's villa outside Spoleto. I took the bus with the cast; Phyllis planned to follow with Alexis in the car. We didn't have directions, and this was

The Spoleto Years (1976-1992)

before the days of cell phones. Halfway to our destination, we stopped at a red light on a dark road. Just as the light changed and the bus pulled away, a group of young men on motorcycles deliberately surrounded Phyllis's car.

Phyllis was in a quandary. It was close to midnight, and she was in danger of getting lost and stranded if she didn't keep up with the bus, but she knew that, in Italy, women didn't dare to speed ahead of men on the road—especially not men driving motorcycles. Should she floor it and risk getting run off the road? She decided to take her chances. She stepped on the gas and luckily managed to catch up with the bus just as it turned off the main road. The motorcyclists let her go, but she was quite frightened. Even today, Italian men are macho on the highway, aggressively tailgating when they want to pass you and sideswiping your car as payback for slowing them down once you finally pull into the right lane.

When Phyllis arrived at the villa, she and Alexis were visibly shaken; Alexis was unusually quiet. "Where's Daddy?" she asked. "I want to go to sleep." Our hosts allowed us to tuck her into bed in one of their spare bedrooms, where she promptly collapsed, exhausted by what had transpired.

The ordeal put a sour note on what would be our final year of involvement in Spoleto. When Gian Carlo Menotti founded the Festival of Two Worlds in Spoleto in 1958 (he founded its companion festival, Spoleto Festival USA, in Charleston, South Carolina, in 1977), no one could have predicted that it would become such an institution. Nor would they have imagined that years later, when he retired, he would leave this extraordinary festival in the hands of his adopted son, Francis "Chip" Menotti. Although he knew little about the arts, Chip was named president of the festival in 1994 and artistic director in 1999. Without its founder, the Spoleto festival soon lost its luster. Worse, Chip undermined its reputation and funding sources.

Shortly after Gian Carlo Menotti died in 2007, the Italian government appointed Giorgio Ferrara head of Spoleto and committed to reviving the festival's original mission of cultural vibrancy and experimentation.

THE LAST IMPRESARIO

It's worth noting that the great Martha Graham left a similarly troubled legacy. Upon her death in 1991, she left control of her dance company to her companion and caretaker for the last years of her life, Ron Protas. Unfortunately, Protas had no background in dance, just as Chip Menotti had no background in performing arts. Both men were removed from their undeserved positions after lengthy and difficult legal battles—resulting in two victories for integrity in the performing arts.

As my reputation expanded and solidified in the early 1980s in Italy, interesting opportunities were on the horizon internationally, lending new challenges to my theatrical palette: presenting La Scala Ballet in the States and a minimalist Broadway musical in Italy.

11
Cross-Cultural Challenges:
Swan Lake to A Chorus Line

La Scala was the first major Western cultural institution I had seen with my own eyes. It was early in my journey from Israel to the West; before, I had seen only the relatively modest opera house în Timișoara. As a result, merely seeing La Scala up close—even without the means to watch a performance there—moved me profoundly. At the same time, my brief proximity to this legendary building seemed to cement my outsider status and reinforce my own insignificance.

But by the late '70s, I was an insider in the theater world—privy to the backstage dramas of various theater administrators. I had learned that the people who held the power in this elite sanctum were politician-bureaucrats appointed by the local mayor, who were largely unconcerned with whether those appointees had the right artistic credentials for administering at such esteemed establishments.

I also learned the hard way that any commitments made by the outgoing regime could be ignored easily by the new guard. In other words, contracts and verbal commitments for tours came with the unspoken understanding that, if their political party got voted out, all bets were off.

The one permanent fixture I encountered at La Scala was Letizia Centinari. Assistant to the *totum factotum,* "*il Sovrintendente,*" she was feisty and personable. Letizia guarded the fort, granting (or refusing to grant) access to her bosses, who changed based on local elections almost as frequently as the wind blowing through the nearby Alps. I first met her in 1978, and, as we developed a working relationship, it became apparent that she was the go-to person to get things done and to ensure that my phone calls were actually returned. She loved to regale me with tales about all the prominent artists who passed through the back door of La Scala, from Toscanini to Pavarotti to Zeffirelli, and I spent hours listening to her stories, knowing that staying on her good side was the best way to ensure access to *il Sovrintendente.*

Every summer, La Scala presented a small number of performances on an outdoor stage at the grand Castello Sforzesco—the massive castle in the heart of Milan, originally built by the Sforza family, who had ruled the city for many years. In 1978, I proposed the Asami Maki Ballet, directed by ballerina and choreographer Maki Asami, to ATER. They responded enthusiastically and booked the company to open at Castello Sforzesco and other major venues in Italy. Since the company had never toured abroad, the city of Tokyo provided a subsidy to the ballet, which meant a summer tour would be possible.

The dates were July 11–13, 1978. After opening night, I invited Dame Asami Maki and her fifty ballerinas to a meal near Castello Sforzesco. We were all seated at a long, narrow table, with Dame Asami at one end and I at the other. "Please sit down," I said. "Make yourselves at home." When everyone had been served wine, I raised my glass, said a few words to welcome them, and congratulated them on their fine performance. I followed it with the traditional Italian toast, "*Cin, cin!*" (pronounced "Chin, chin!").

I was baffled when my toast produced a brief stunned silence, followed by embarrassed giggling all around the table. What had I said

Cross-Cultural Challenges: Swan Lake to A Chorus Line

wrong? We continued the meal, while I silently tried to figure out my faux pas. I had done my utmost to be a gracious host. After dessert, I raised my glass again to say a few final words. "I hope to see you again in Italy soon. *Cin, cin!*" By this point, the ballerinas had enjoyed the Italian wine and were noticeably more at ease, so their laughter was no longer restrained. Some of them almost fell out of their chairs laughing. I knew I had said something hilarious, so I asked them, "What's the matter? What does *cin, cin* mean in Japanese?" Nobody would tell me. Several days later, when the tour reached Nice, the administrator of the company pulled me to the side. Hesitantly and very respectfully, she told me I should never say *"cin cin"* to Japanese people because *"cin"* meant "penis," and *"cin cin"* meant . . . a small one! After that mortifying experience, I became even more mindful that words can mean very different things in different languages.

When I shared my newfound wisdom with the Italians, I received varied responses, from surprise to a casual *"certo"* ("of course"). Despite my initial lack of worldliness, or maybe because of it, the Italians continued to welcome me into their inner sanctum as a close friend, exuding warmth and conviviality. With their enthusiasm and friendship, I became more confident about proposing ideas. After several years of orchestrating tours of select dance companies such as the San Francisco Ballet, the Houston Ballet, and the Pennsylvania Ballet for Italian and French festivals, I proposed the idea of bringing the La Scala Opera to the U.S. I had worked with Carlo Badini while he was president of ATER—the powerful umbrella organization for the most important opera houses in northern Italy—when he first started bringing dance companies to the festivals. He had befriended me and treated me like a son, so, when I heard that he had been appointed *Sovrintendente* of La Scala, I didn't waste a moment before knocking on his door.

Badini was very friendly but hesitant to let a young, unseasoned impresario undertake a U.S. tour of the world's most prestigious opera company. Our negotiations stretched over at least three years. Sometimes he would summon me for a meeting, and I would rush to the airport, board a plane, and show up in his fabled office by 10 the next morning. In retrospect, he probably wanted me to prove my dedication to the project. On one occasion, I got home from Europe—and then returned the next day because he invited me to attend an important opening at La Scala. Needless to say, my family wasn't happy. Still, I saw it as an opportunity I couldn't ignore.

As it turned out, I was right. When I arrived at La Scala, Badini greeted me warmly. It wasn't long before he said, "*Caro Piter,*" his trademark cigar in the corner of his mouth, "*Perché prima non porti il nostro balletto negli States? Mi stanno tra i piedi.*" ("Dear Peter, why don't you bring the Scala *Ballet* to the States first? They are in my way.") Before he would commit to touring an opera, he wanted me to tour Zeffirelli's brand-new production of *Swan Lake*. I agreed to explore the possibility, my heart nearly bursting out of my chest with excitement.

He escorted me to the Royal Box for the opening performance that evening. It was June 1985—almost 20 years since my first pilgrimage to Milan. Here I was, now seated next to Misha Baryshnikov in the Royal Box of La Scala. Misha, now artistic director of ABT, was seeking new dancers for the company, while I was contemplating a tour of the U.S. and Canada for the La Scala Ballet. (Misha later hired the extraordinary ballerina Alessandra Ferri.) We reminisced about his performance of Twyla Tharp at Nervi, when he spontaneously altered his movements to incorporate the rain.

As I sat watching this grand production, my days in Timișoara felt like a lifetime ago. I couldn't help but smile. I had finally made it *inside*. I had a deep sense of belonging, of cultural and emotional connection, of shared sensibility and values that transcended my previous experiences. And there was music. That magical evening, it seemed that the orchestra of La Scala played only for me.

Being offered a chance to tour the La Scala production of Zeffirelli's dramatic and controversial ballet with world-famous Lorin Maazel

Cross-Cultural Challenges: Swan Lake to A Chorus Line

(1930–2014) sounded glamorous, but reality soon set in. Shepherding a company of two hundred-twenty-five people, not to mention nine fifty-three-foot trailer trucks for sets and costumes, around the U.S. would be daunting. As I watched the elaborate production unfold, my reverie gave way to the realization that transporting this massive crew was going to be a producer's nightmare. Not only was it cost-prohibitive (who would pay their fees?), but the logistics were formidable. They became even more problematic when I heard the Italian dancers' union's unrealistic demands. I would have to balance all this with the irrational "artistic" requirements of Sergio Barzotto, the ballet's emotionally unstable administrator. The proposal was tempting, despite its hurdles, but I still questioned my sanity in even considering it. I told myself that, upon returning to New York, I would contact a few theaters, but it was unlikely they would have the interest, the funds, or the available dates to make the tour feasible, which would resolve my internal debate for me.

Much to my surprise—and in some respects, dismay—I found three venues that wanted to buy the show for one week each for the summer of 1986: The National Arts Center in Ottawa, the magnificent Fox Theater in Atlanta, and the Opera House in San Francisco. To make the tour viable and get this enormous production to the West Coast, I had to find a theater willing to host a week of performances somewhere in middle America. The festival at the MUNI in St. Louis came just in time. But an outdoor venue in a municipal park would require a different set—God help us! We would have to build this additional set, which would also have to be approved by Maestro Zeffirelli himself. The technical director of La Scala, Giorgio Cristini, flew in from Milano to discuss the project, and I accompanied him to the MUNI, where he took measurements, assessed the stage and its surroundings, and hoped to obtain permission to construct a special outdoor set specifically for this venue. The major decor pieces were *six* 50-foot columns in *vetroresina* (fiberglass). I still hate that word! It put the entire project into deficit, which caused a strain on my marriage! The massive ballroom columns for the first and third act would have to be built at Cinecittà, the studios of the RAI Italian TV networks and film industry. (RAI, which originally stood for Radio Audizioni Italiane and now stands for Radiotelevisione Italiana, is Italy's national public broadcasting company, owned by the Ministry of Economy and Finance.) Giorgio intimated that Zeffirelli was less than enthused about bringing his "masterpiece to the hinterland" and staging an outdoor production of a piece intended only for the sacred stage of La Scala.

I was hoping for help from my *padrino*, Badini, but he had his own issues with Zeff. With an ironic smile, he told me, "*Fai da te, Piter!*" ("You are on your own, Peter.") He warned that sending Zeff a case of champagne might not be enough to do the trick. "*Perché non vai da Zeff? Il suo posto ti piacerà!*" "Why don't you go see Zeff? You will like his place!"

I had traveled back and forth so much already that I was loath to board yet another plane just to coax Zeffirelli into conceding to an open-air performance of his fabled *Swan Lake*, and one that would leave me grappling with the burden of another set. But now that I had contracts with three theaters, I was afraid that reneging would destroy my reputation. ("You're only as good as your last show" held true even before performances were immortalized and always accessible for playback on the Internet.) What's more, I was still young and ambitious—and more than a bit curious about visiting Zeff at his villa in Positano on the Amalfi coast.

Giorgio and I flew to the noisy, chaotic Naples airport, where Zeff's driver greeted us and whisked us to his grand four-level Villa TreVille.[1] The entrance was hidden in the rocks, and we had to descend about sixty steps, surrounded by bougainvillea, to reach the reception area, where four handsome, well-built young men in shorts were playing table tennis. We were greeted by the house *maggiordomo*, a middle-aged woman who offered us drinks while we waited for the Maestro under the grand gazebo overlooking the sea.

"*Venite a guardare i giardini. Son belli in primavera,*" she said. "Come see the gardens. They're beautiful in spring."

Cross-Cultural Challenges: Swan Lake to A Chorus Line

We descended to the next level, where Zeff greeted us and treated us to an alfresco lunch of *spaghetti vongole*. He was casually dressed and a bit reserved. Giorgio introduced me as the American producer of the tour.

"Now to you I must to speak English? It is not very good!" Zeffirelli exclaimed disdainfully.

"No, Maestro," I responded. "*l'Italiano va benissimo*."

His mood changed.

With the prospect of an open-air presentation, Zeff had to rethink how he would engage the audience without a proscenium indoor stage. Luckily, Giorgio had already become an ally and had a proposal that seemed to appeal to Zeff, who was suddenly and surprisingly easygoing and agreeable. We talked about how invested he was in his *Swan Lake*, his first foray into the world of ballet, and since he felt that his reputation was at stake, he would not compromise any aspect of the set, regardless of cost.

The production's centerpiece was a group of columns, tapered at the bottom, so it appeared they didn't touch the ground. The six used indoors were from La Scala, but six new ones would have to be built by Cinecittà for 200 million lira (about $100,000) for the outdoor performances at The MUNI, shipped to New York and trucked to St. Louis, only to be destroyed after the tour! Adding to the overall expense was the $75 daily for food that all 110 dancers received per their union's requirements. With the large crew and the numerous dancers with their high per diem, there was no way I could contain costs. As I sat across from him, I started wondering if this made any sense. I was glad I'd had the experience of visiting Zeff, but was this tour worth the risk?

After lunch, we moved to the fourth level, where Zeff showed us a cave carved into the stone, with a huge marble bathtub of three by six meters that, he explained, had been flown in by an American Army helicopter. It was a set in itself, made of polished Carrara marble. Zeff was gracious, offering to extend our stay to let us enjoy a siesta, but we were eager to return to Naples to catch our plane, and we didn't want to overstay our welcome.[1]

Despite my reservations, we went ahead with the tour. From the beginning, it presented hurdles not only with the sets but with the dancers. Carla Fracci was the star, and though she was respected in Italy, she was problematic. She would partner only with muscular men who could easily carry her as she often lacked the strength and technique required for her roles. On top of that, she often arrived late for rehearsals and would

Cross-Cultural Challenges: Swan Lake to A Chorus Line

disappear with a female dancer after performances, while her spouse, Beppe Menegatti, went off with the guys, leaving their teenage son behind to fend for himself. I put her on notice twice for arriving late to rehearsals, and then I fired her. At least here, Badini, my padrino, backed me.

The press was ambivalent about La Scala's *Swan Lake*, as I had expected them to be, but I was betting on Americans responding enthusiastically to Zeffirelli's tour de force—and I was right. Audiences loved his over-the-top spectacle. Unfortunately, all I could think about was how much the "support" staff and the endless overtime hours of load-in and load-out were costing. *Pazienza!* Expenses for the four-week tour were way over budget, resulting in a significant loss for me.[2]

Fortunately, I had a profitable production of *A Chorus Line* touring Italy at the same time. In the '70s and '80s, the most effective way to book tours of Italy was to start by securing one of the country's two most prestigious festivals—Menotti's Spoleto or the International Festival in Nervi. In 1986, after securing *A Chorus Line* engagement in Nervi, I was approached by the administrator of Torre del Lago, the Puccini Festival, to book three performances. When I quoted him a fee, he asked if it was per performance or for all three. Without missing a beat, I responded with *faux* indignation: "*Maestro, per favore, come si può immaginare questo cachet per tre recite? Certamente per spettacolo!*" ("Maestro, please, how can you imagine that price for three performances? It's certainly per performance!")

"*Ma certamente, Dottor Klein...*"

And just like that, the contract was sealed for three times the amount I had anticipated. During these wonderful years, the Italian theaters were flush with state and local subsidies, which they wanted to spend entirely. This way their budget for the following year would be just as high or higher and not be cut.

The show was a first—not only for Italy, but for Europe. It was also the first musical performed at the Puccini Festival at Torre del Lago on the Tuscany coast; until then, only operas had been performed at this high-end and very prestigious Festival. I meant no disrespect to my much-beloved composer, but the audience was a different matter!

I had planned to attend the opening night of *Swan Lake* in Ottawa and then catch a plane to Nervi the day before *A Chorus Line* opened, in order to help set up. Disastrously, our company manager got sick during the Ottawa performances of *Swan Lake* and couldn't travel to the third and most challenging stop on the tour: the open-air show at the MUNI in St. Louis. When we could find no last-minute replacement for him, I knew I had no choice but to do his job myself. The week-long engagement of *Swan Lake* ended in Ottawa the evening of Sunday, July 6, 1986.

The two DC3 pilots and I had to load the cargo, which filled up so much of the plane that the pilots could only reach the cockpit through the windows. They told us they were required to have two exits for safety reasons, but to my relief and astonishment, they gallantly ignored regulations for the *gran' balletto*. They were good sports and wired ahead to St. Louis to have ladders ready so they would be able to disembark through the cockpit windows. "Obliging the arts!" they assured me. I got three hours sleep that night, but it was sufficient for a forty-year-old "youngster" like me. This was especially remarkable to someone who had grown up in a rigid and oppressive Communist country, where there was no flexibility in the application of laws and regulations—at least not without money changing hands. These young, spirited pilots were excited about our production and eager to help. Of course, this was in pre-terrorism days—it's hard to imagine their rule-bending in today's world. As for the other fifty-three-foot containers with the specially built *vetroresina* grand set pieces, they were already at the St. Louis theater.

I was relieved but still exhausted and terrified that we wouldn't be ready for opening night the following evening. I tried to convince myself that *A Chorus Line* opening in Nervi would go well even without me. Unfortunately, I didn't really believe it.

My mind kept wandering back to a near calamity that occurred in July 1980, when I escorted Russian ballet dancer Alexander Godunov

Cross-Cultural Challenges: Swan Lake to A Chorus Line

(1949–1995) from a performance in southern France to Tel Aviv after he defected from the USSR. Because of the extraordinary success of his sold-out shows, we added a performance in Nice, even though we knew the connection would be tight since he had an important TV interview scheduled in Tel Aviv less than twenty-four hours later. After the last Nice show, Godunov, his ballet mistress/sidekick, Elena Tchernichova (1942–2015), and I had a sumptuous dinner with French impresario Youly Algaroff (1918–1995) at Le Chantecler, which stayed open past midnight for us. Then we hit the road to Genoa to catch the 7:00 a.m. flight to Rome, and then on to Tel Aviv.

We left around 2:00 a.m. I assumed traffic would be minimal in the middle of the night, so, as we rode along the Grand Corniche, the winding cliffside expressway with spectacular seaside views, we were confident that we would have plenty of time to make our flight from Genoa. But no sooner had we reached the Italian side of the border than we encountered a heavy storm, with lightning, thunder, and water coming down in torrents. The road was blocked. Dozens of cars had stopped in the tunnels carved into the mountains, and parts of the highway were completely flooded. We were forced to pull off the road. We finally arrived in Genoa at 6:00 a.m. to find the airport closed due to flooding. It finally opened at 8:00 a.m., and we were informed that the fight would depart at 10:00 a.m.

"This can't be!" I told the airport staff. "It's essential that we catch the TWA flight from Rome to Tel Aviv! I'd like to speak to the airport manager."

"Sorry, sir," the manager said. "There's absolutely nothing we can do. You are lucky that the flight wasn't canceled."

"Can you call ahead to see if there is another flight that we can catch?" I begged. I thought about calling the TV station, but I was afraid they would cancel the interview. I couldn't risk it.

We finally boarded the flight. While in the air, I walked up to the cockpit and asked if I could speak to the pilot. I went straight to the captain and asked if he could radio ahead and have the plane wait in Fiumicino, Rome, for our arrival from Genoa.

"*Ci penso io*," he assured me, "Don't worry. I'll take care of it."

He found out the TWA flight to Tel Aviv was just leaving the gate. He explained that a famous ballet star was trying to make the connection. Fortunately the TWA captain, a lover of ballet, got permission from the Fiumicino control tower to stop on the way to the runway. Godunov and Tchernichova were taken off the Alitalia flight before reaching the gate and to a waiting airport car; then they were whisked to the TWA plane, conveniently positioned alongside ours. *Whew!* It was a well-choreographed *pas de deux* in which one bird landed while the other prepared for takeoff.

As I reflect upon these international backstage/offstage dramas, I realize how much more restriction we live with now, particularly when it comes to movement around the globe. It strikes me as particularly sad when I recall the excitement of bringing the arts across borders in those days. What a sense of optimism and possibility we felt. How we believed in bridging differences among cultures through a shared passion for music and dance. Even governments shared our enthusiasm, occasionally providing generous state funding for culture.

I stayed on the Alitalia plane, picked up the bags for the three of us, and took a later flight. Godunov made the TV appearance, and ticket sales soared. That's not to say that it was always smooth sailing. Two years later, I was flying from Caracas to New York with Godunov and Jaqueline Bisset, whom he was dating, when we encountered another airport drama. The Caracas customs staff refused to let us board the only Pan Am flight that day, with the excuse that Godunov didn't have the "necessary tax documents." Overhearing the staff's conversation, I realized they just wanted more time to gawk at gorgeous, famous Jacqueline Bisset.

I immediately contacted my friend Jojo Naim, the one who had flown Phyllis and me on his four-seater from Caracas to Isla el Gran Roque for a day in 1976. Jojo and I devised an alternate plan in case we encountered the same problem when we returned the next day. He would surreptitiously fly us to the much-friendlier Aruba, a thirty-minute flight, and,

Cross-Cultural Challenges: Swan Lake to A Chorus Line

from there, we could fly to New York. Ultimately, the American Embassy contacted the authorities at the airport and made sure Godunov was allowed to board, so we didn't need Jojo's help after all.

The following day, I returned from St. Louis to New York, departing again that evening on the last flight for Italy—the opening of *A Chorus Line* in Nervi loomed. I arrived at Malpensa, Milan's airport, after having caught a few hours' sleep on the plane. From there, I rented a car and drove three hours along the winding highways through the mountains to Nervi, east of Genoa. Just as I arrived, crossing through the ornate gates of the park, I found the Italian and American crews at each other's throats.

"I know the production!" exclaimed the American.

"No, il palcoscenico e mio, lo conosco meglio di voi! . . ." ("The stage is mine. I know it better.")

By noon, setting up the stage for the evening's much-anticipated opening performance had not yet begun! Usually, preparing the stage started early in the morning before the midday heat. It was now close to 1:00 p.m. The sun was blazing down, and the Italians were about to take their sacred lunch break, which would last for two hours. I pulled the two technical directors aside and insisted that they put aside personal and national pride, promising each an incentive.

A Chorus Line was the first Broadway musical to come to the Nervi festival. It was a much-talked-about event throughout Europe, and media from all over Europe were attending. I was terrified that a cultural collision between the crews would damage my reputation with Nervi. Overcome by some premonition of disaster, I rushed to my hotel and spent all afternoon combing through the Genoa phone book and making calls, trying to find a local lawyer who wasn't affiliated with either of the two major political parties—the Democrazia Cristiana in power in Rome, and the PCI or Partito Comunista Italiano, governing most of the Northern Italian regions. My fear was that this fight between the two crews would undermine the intricate lighting of the stage and the functioning of the sound system, the show would go terribly, and Levrero, the festival's administrator, would simply refuse to pay me or my cast and crew. My many years of life under Communism had taught me that laws and contracts were not things that officials always adhered to, and at least having a lawyer not connected to the government gave me some small sense of security.

I walked onto the stage at 9 p.m. and saw that the dance floor was not yet taped down—a step that's usually completed in the first hour of setup. My anxiety rising, I took the microphone from the sound man and signaled the electrician to throw the follow-spot on me. I cleared my throat, forced a smile, and began assuring the audience in Italian that we were *almost* ready and to bear with us for just a bit longer.

"Please be patient," I implored the audience. "We'll start soon."

The stage manager approached me and insisted that the crew needed another full hour. An hour delay would be suicide, even for Italians, who are famously tardy. I told him we absolutely *had* to start by 9:30. The major technical challenge was the scenery, which required sophisticated and elaborate lighting that used a lot of kilowatts. There wasn't enough electrical juice left to power the sound system.

We started at 9:35. The Italians had trouble understanding the English, and after an hour, the audience started leaving in droves. I had flashbacks to my very first production at Hunter College, when the actor's accent drove some of the audience away. Now, of course, the stakes were much higher. The final number, "One," would be a crowd-pleaser—of that I was sure—but there was a seemingly interminable monologue that came just before it. Whatever power and dramatic meaning the monologue held for American audiences would be lost on the Italian crowd. Hoping to avoid this final road bump, I raced to the stage manager and begged that he cut the sequence and direct the cast and crew to go directly into "One." He refused, stating that it was beyond his authority to cut any portion of a show. Of course, when "One" finally began, the audience that had managed to stick out the show did enjoy the number. Nonetheless, it was safe to say the evening

Cross-Cultural Challenges: Swan Lake to A Chorus Line

had not been a success. Director Livero left after the show without even saying goodnight. I returned to my hotel room that night exhausted but mentally preparing for battle.

The next morning, I met my lawyer, Ottavio Bruni, on the lovely, shaded terrace of my room at the Astor Hotel. I had my appointment with Mr. Levrero at his office at the opera house before noon, where he was supposed to hand me the financial documents that would authorize the local bank to release the funds for the festival's payment to me. I was concerned that he would not honor the payment, that he would cast aside the contract and use the success (or lack of success) of the show as the litmus test for whether services had been rendered. Whether this was rational or some mild paranoia induced by my years in Romania, I don't know, but I expected a confrontation and a possible implosion of my reputation at a festival that had nurtured my fledgling career and that I and my family had loved for so long. On the way to the opera house, we stopped for the morning papers. To my complete astonishment, both *Corriere della Sera* and *La Repubblica* had run rave reviews of the show! So had the local paper, *XIX Secolo*. I realized what had happened: using my track record—and the press that my good friend Giovanni Soresi had released regarding the artistic merit of the show—as a guide, from ABT to the Boston Ballet and many others, the Italian critics had simply assumed another hit and had written their reviews accordingly—in advance!

Raves in hand, Bruni and I walked into Levrero's office. Without a word, I placed the newspapers on his desk. It didn't matter that we both knew that the reviews were a misrepresentation, to say the least, of the previous night's fiasco. The press had heralded the production a success—which I knew held power. However annoyed or frustrated Levrero might have been, he handed me the financial papers. I heaved an enormous sigh of relief and headed to the bank.

After Nervi, the company and I traveled to the Puccini Festival, where the show was an *actual* success. The rest of the tour was also well-received, and *A Chorus Line* was ultimately hailed as an American masterpiece. The local Italian critics were suddenly enthralled by musical theater, which had no equivalent in Italy.

The public, however, was skeptical about the merit of *A Chorus Line*. This was most Italian theater-goers' first exposure to Broadway, and they didn't respond well to all the talking. They were used to opera, which is entirely sung and allows you to enjoy the music regardless of what is being "said." At the time, I was so excited about bringing *A Chorus Line* to Italy that I underestimated how foreign it would be for the audience. It may also have been the themes of the show, which, in hindsight, required some cultural knowledge of the American theater world and the struggles of its performers. The show was, even for America, extremely modern; its focus on the personal woes and triumphs of a set of auditioning dancers was perhaps too culturally far afield for Italian audiences. In general, they were more open to visually contemporary performances than to musicals, even with subtitles appearing to the side of the stage.

When you speak the language of two cultures, you sometimes overlook the nuances and sensibilities that separate them. We offered realism to opera fans. It was simply too big a leap. In turn, I was offering a "vaudeville" production of *Swan Lake* to the Americans. Only with some distance from this summer can I appreciate the ironies and challenges of cultural differences or clashes as well as the audience's difficulties in grasping nuances.

After all that, I never did tour the La Scala opera. Badini did in fact grant me the right, but when I began to put the tour together, word got out, and he received some angry phone calls from The Kennedy Center. It was their right, they felt, as an opera house, and one of the major cultural representatives of the American theater, to make such an enormous exchange—and most definitely *not* the right of an independent producer. The Met soon joined the chorus of complaints, and Badini called to request that I cancel the tour. Deeply apologetic, he said, *"Piter,* instead, bring a company to Italy, and La Scala will present it and pay

Cross-Cultural Challenges: Swan Lake to A Chorus Line

for it." And, so, I brought the National Ballet of Canada, and with La Scala presenting it in Milan, we had sold-out performances at the Teatro Lirico. Certainly, it was a loving and adequate compensation for my disappointment, but it will always feel like a dream permanently deferred, a circle not quite completed.

In 1986, I received a phone call from the office of Monaco's Caroline, Princess of Hanover. I was surprised and pleased. She had heard about

my successful U.S. and Canadian tour of the La Scala Ballet and hoped I would help her with one of her own pet projects. Caroline was passionate about reviving the new Ballets de Monte Carlo, heir to the famous Ballets Russes de Monte Carlo, as a tribute to her mother, Princess Grace (better remembered by Americans as Grace Kelly). The group had received mixed reviews after its launch in 1985 and was facing an uphill battle to establish themselves as a world-class company. I was happy to sign on.

I visited the opera house in Monaco to see the ballet, and was captivated by the exquisite costumes, which had come from the Ballets Russes and were designed by Massine for the Diaghilev/Nijinsky repertoire. My thoughts drifted back to Simon Semenoff, the man who introduced me to the Hurok office, setting my life course in motion so many years ago. He would have been thrilled to know that I was bringing the world-famous ballet company with whom he had danced in 1942, back to the United States forty-five years later.

And this wasn't my only emotional connection to Princess Grace. She had commissioned my Viennese cousin Robert Dornhelm to do a documentary film in 1977 called *Children of Theater Street*, which examined the rigorous competition among young Russian dancers for a spot in the elite Kirov Ballet.

Robert offered to make a brief infomercial to help me publicize the tour. Robert's parents were the relatives who'd welcomed my family to Vienna when we left Romania so many years earlier, so sharing this project with him had special meaning for me.

I knew bringing the company to the States so soon after its launch was risky, but in the tour publicity, I emphasized its legacy and the glamour of Monte Carlo. What's more, the Diaghilev/Nijinsky repertoire had been absent from the American stage for a long time, and I suspected fans might be nostalgic for it. Box office sales proved that I was right. There was an enthusiastic audience for Les Ballets Russes de Monte Carlo. It was cathartic to experience threads from my past and present intertwining. It was also a relief to think that my investment in Zeffirelli's *Swan Lake*, which had been such a financial strain, had at least paid off in the press it had given me—it was, after all, what had prompted Princess Caroline's interest.

Political winds in Hong Kong also favored new possibilities in the '80s for American performing artists. In retrospect, I am particularly fascinated with Martha Graham's political thrust in view of our present struggles. I was privileged to present the Graham company with Martha in attendance in 1989 at the Hong Kong Arts Festival. I did not know at the time that this would be her last international tour with her company. Although Mark Franko, author of *Martha Graham in Love and War*, believes that her creative force was dampened by this time, the program selected was representative of the breadth of her work. Graham expressed the politicization of her time choreographically. Although she choreographed much of her work in the '40s, the thrust of her work represented a freedom that is still powerful today.[3]

Interestingly, although this was my first time touring with Martha, I had developed a close relationship with Pearl Lang, whom I'd toured in Europe and Israel ten years earlier. Agnes de Mille had idealized Martha. She wrote a book of her early dance childhood entitled *Where the Wings Grow*, based on Martha's directive to all students of the dance to "... stand proudly ..." Thus, when, I finally worked with Martha on tour, it took some time to separate the myth from her as a person. At this point in her life, she was very appreciative of this opportunity, even though she had toured around the world. Undoubtedly, she was now looking back rather than forward.

I toured Eric Hawkins, her dance partner and husband, in 1979. He and Martha had divorced in 1954. I presented him at the Nervi festival with his choreography, *Parson Weems and the Cherry Tree*, based on the tale of George Washington and the cherry tree, which premiered in 1976. The dance is about George Washington's father, who taught him the importance of truth. Clearly, it was a propaganda piece for

American democracy—which I did not consider at the time—and is particularly ironic as we are now living once again in a political climate of distorted truths. The dance was not received with enthusiasm by the Italians, as they seemed unable to relate to the importance of truth from our first President.

12

The Mafia Reigns

In 1980, I saw the revival of *West Side Story* at the Minskoff, and I knew right away that I wanted to tour it. I had seen the film in 1965. I was a nineteen-year-old in Israel and just forming my own hazy impression of America. *West Side Story* had left a lasting impression. Now a full-fledged American citizen, producing the show had even greater meaning for me.

I contacted the Nederlanders, who had produced the revival. They directed me to their general manager, Ralph Roseman, and his colleague, Charlotte Wilcox. Everyone was enthusiastic about my proposal for a tour of France and Italy starting at the Nervi festival in July of 1981, and a contract was soon signed. In retrospect, it's hard to believe it took twenty-four years for the smash Broadway hit from 1957 to fly across the Atlantic.[1]

We began preparations in early 1981 with great excitement on both sides of the ocean. Jerome Robbins was set to direct rehearsals in New York, but to my dismay, his office called in mid-April to say he didn't have time after all. In fact, he wanted to postpone the tour for a year!

"We have a signed contract," I reminded them. "The theaters have already begun to sell tickets!" I tried to keep my voice calm, but my reputation was on the line. Canceling would be *brutta figura* (something unacceptable), in the eyes of my Italian partners.

Jerry remained adamant that he had no time to rehearse. I quickly realized my only option was to take legal action. I served him with papers claiming direct and consequential damages of $3 million. Three days later, I got word that he had delegated rehearsals to Richard Caceres, a talented dancer who worked for him.

In St. Barts the following winter we saw Jerry and a young lover wearing matching striped bathing trunks, on the beach near the Guanahani Hotel. He barely acknowledged me, and it was clear in that instant that Jerry was unaccustomed to *not* getting his way. Still, it was a disappointment to see him react like that.

Jerry was the artistic equivalent of a "made man" in gangster parlance, and that meant no one should dare to challenge him. Breaking with tradition always has consequences. Perhaps my courage grew out of naïveté—and the same proud, rebellious streak that had punctuated many of my actions. (It's worth noting that I went on to tour *West Side Story* a number of times in the twenty years that followed, without complications. Touring non-Broadway union productions drew less scrutiny from Robbins and Bernstein foundations than Broadway union productions.

Our six-week tour of Italy was a marvelous success. After it ended in Palermo, as my tours usually did, we played Monte Carlo. The Nederlanders themselves showed up and joined us for dinner; Mrs. Nederlander was lavishly draped in a mink fur jacket despite the sultry summer evenings on the Riviera.

The ticket sales were so strong that Princess Grace herself asked us to extend the Monte Carlo engagement for a second week. All but two members of the sixty-member company eagerly agreed, but it wasn't to be. Because I had purchased the full Broadway production of *West Side Story*, Actors' Equity Association (AEA) was involved, and they refused to allow the extension, even after I offered financial compensation to the two cast members who wanted to leave.

The Mafia Reigns

As a result, fifty-eight company members had to give up a week's stay in fabulous Monte Carlo, earnings of $1,100 apiece a week—a lot of money in 1981—and lodgings in beautiful single rooms overlooking the Mediterranean. Union votes were private, and two performers had not wanted to stay. The Union ruled that the contract could not be altered without unanimous consent. And so, all of the fifty-eight company members returned to New York to stand on unemployment lines for $95 a week. Actors' Equity had actually acted against the interests of their own members. Charlotte Wilcox, who now runs her own company managing major Broadway shows, was as frustrated as I was. It was absolutely baffling that the union would rule to deprive performers of good pay and a wonderful experience. The incident reinforced my view that unions sometimes develop a stranglehold on their members, destroying opportunities for the very people whose careers they are supposed to protect. It held an echo of the brutal and nonsensical bureaucracy of Communism, which always professed to be acting in the interests of its people.

A few years later, I encountered a foe more formidable—and much more menacing—than Actors' Equity. It began when two businessmen from Naples contacted me. They were fans of the American TV series *Fame*, which in Italy went by the name *Saranno Famosi*. *Fame* starred Gene Anthony Ray (1962–2003) in the lead role of Leroy, and the two men wanted to bring the popular actor to Italy. I proposed that we mount a kind of mini-version of *"Fame,"* using some of the music and choreography, and hiring George Faison to direct. I suggested the title *"Buona Fortuna!"* and soon, we had finalized the details.

Next, I brought Gene to Italy to appear on several popular talk shows in order to build excitement for the upcoming tour. One sunny day, we were walking down the Via del Corso in Rome, when some teenagers recognized Gene. Seconds later, the four of us—Gene, the two Italian promoters, and I—were mobbed by hundreds of kids desperate to get his autograph. Alarmed, store owners started frantically pulling down their shutters to protect their shops. We took refuge in the Ritz Hotel and escaped through a back entrance. My contacts were certain the tour would be a sellout because of Gene's apparent popularity, but they had minimal experience in show business. I remained less certain, the excitement of that afternoon notwithstanding.

Mostly, I was concerned that my two clients had not done the legwork involved in building an audience for a tour—the publicity and promotion. They had already invested substantially, and perhaps they had run out of capital, but whatever the reason, I doubted the seats would be filled. To my pleasure and delight, my new friend, Michele Andreano, a freshly minted lawyer, was with me from the beginning, experiencing firsthand the challenges of show business.

Gene and the other twenty-five cast members arrived in Milan for the opening night, in Como. The bus showed up late, and the hotel had not been booked. We were off to an inauspicious start. Worse, we opened to an audience of five hundred in the massive 13,000-seat Como Stadium, making the optics dreadful. Ticket sales did not pick up for the remaining three weeks. As a result, the promoters paid me only half of the amount guaranteed by our contract.

When we reached Sorrento on the Amalfi coast, I confronted the promoters. I told them we could perform no more shows without full payment. They insisted they wouldn't pay one lira more *unless* we performed. The standoff escalated into an argument in front of our hotel. The heat was unbearable that afternoon, and the whole scene had become nightmarish. Then, I saw my contacts give each other a subtle wink and step away from me. Suddenly, I heard the roar of an engine and looked up in horror to see a car speeding straight toward me. The driver actually tried to jump the curb to run me down! By sheer luck, the sidewalk was very high, and the car careened off the edge. Meanwhile, both promoters had vanished. My heart pounding, I hurried inside, packed my belongings, and raced through the kitchen to the back door of the hotel. I only wished Michele had been with me then.

The Mafia Reigns

Alone, I took the first taxi I could find to Ercolano, where I spent the night. From there, I called the tour manager and my friend, the multi-talented Casey McClellan, and arranged to have Gene and the rest of the group depart Sorrento for Roma immediately, and then board the first available Pan Am flight back to New York. The gods of show biz must have been looking down on me to secure some thirty seats for the following day.

I breathed a sigh of relief when everyone was finally on board, but the tour was a financial fiasco. Normally, I refused to be derailed, but this was different. This was the Mob. I was lucky to be in one piece. It would be many years before I felt comfortable enough to work with private individuals in Italy again.

Although my experiences in Palermo were generally positive, Mafia stories continued to haunt me. Still, the beauty of the country, the opportunities to work with the prestigious Festival at Parco della Favorita, and the summer residence of the famous Teatro Massimo (where, speaking of the Mafia, parts of the movie *The Godfather* were filmed) were hard to resist. I had also developed some meaningful friendships over the years, and I felt confident that the risk was minimal.

After bringing Alvin Ailey, The San Francisco Ballet, *A Chorus Line*, and *West Side Story* to Palermo, in 1992, I proposed bringing The Joffrey Ballet to Palermo. I had already successfully toured the company in Germany the previous winter; the notices had been great, and Teatro Massimo eagerly agreed to the idea.

Parco della Favorita is an enchanting city park with an outdoor stage, flanked by Monte Pellegrino and Monte Gallo. It is ideally located on the road from Palermo to the seaside resort village of Mondello. It can be reached by a number of tree-lined avenues leading from the center of Palermo. The area is renowned for its historic sites, its numerous Art Nouveau villas, and for having one of the most celebrated shorelines of Sicily—the backdrop for the annual *World Festival on the Beach*. Palermo is also known for its *Opera dei Pupi*—the opera of puppets—which I presented as part of the "Italy in Houston" event in 1986. The *Opera dei Pupi* presents dramas as violent and passionate as those one expects in a Mafia hangout.

We arrived in Palermo on July 18, 1992. The next evening, I was enjoying *fettucine frutti di mare* and a nice bottle of Lamuri Reserva at the Hotel Centrale with my new friend Gerald Arpino (1923–2008), partner of Robert Joffrey (1930–1988), before the 9 p.m. dress rehearsal. Suddenly, a massive explosion shook the hotel windows. Despite our alarm, no one else seemed unnerved by the blast, so we cautiously resumed our dinner.

Gerry, who had a dry sense of humor, said, "Peter, I know you're in theater, but you should try to keep the drama on the stage—not on the streets."

The next morning, we read in the *Giornale di Sicilia* that anti-Mafia magistrate Paolo Borsellino (1940–1992) had been killed by a car bomb—just three hundred feet from us.

Even now, Borsellino—who died just fifty-seven days after his friend and fellow anti-Mafia magistrate Giovanni Falcone was assassinated—is remembered as a hero in the government's battle to end the mob's stranglehold on Italy. (Experts peg Mafia-related costs to Italian merchants at 30 billion Euros—or $35 billion—a year. "Protection fees" for businesses range from 100 to 10,000 Euros a month, and those who refuse to pay risk intimidation, threats, having their stores burned down, or worse. Ironically, businesses that pay the *"pizzo"* say they don't feel any safer.)[2]

Our opening night had to be canceled, and we did three shows instead of four.

I tried to call Phyllis in New York, but I couldn't find a free telephone anywhere in the hotel. When I finally got to a phone, the line was continually busy. Although I knew Mafia "hits" were not uncommon, I was rattled. I told myself that, after surviving the Six-Day War in Israel, I could handle this, but I began to feel as if I were in my body cast again, unable to move freely. What's more, I was responsible for the group I had brought here, and despite assurances from my local contacts, I was

The Mafia Reigns

worried about what might happen next, especially after my experience in Sorrento just three years earlier.

I felt encouraged when I heard that the other three shows we had scheduled would go on. I wanted to get on a plane as fast as possible, but I reminded myself that this was about Borsellino—it had nothing to do with us. I knew the theater would pay me, and I had an obligation not just to protect the Joffrey dancers but to make sure they got to dance—and get paid for their work.

Ultimately, the Joffrey performances were very well received. Nevertheless, I was hugely relieved to get the dancers—and myself—home to New York. Whenever I was on my way home from the airport, my two little girls would wait to hear the key in the lock and then run to the front door to greet me. This time, Phyllis and I embraced as if I were a long-lost war veteran. She had heard the news but had not betrayed any anxiety to the children. From then on, I followed the news stories covering Sicily's struggle to rein in the Mafia, wondering if I would have to cross the island off my list, along with Sorrento. Ten years later, in 2002, with the collaboration of my long-time friend and colleague, Marilla Simonini, I brought a *non*-Broadway production of *West Side Story* to Palermo and Pistoia. No fireworks this time in Palermo! By contrast, in Pistoia, not far from Verona, the outdoor production in the piazza in front of City Hall was pure joy—a true contemporary *Romeo and Juliet*.

13
Liza

In 2007, a debonair-but-shady Italian high-roller named Gianni Filippini got in touch with me. He claimed to have access to significant money. He knew that Liza Minnelli had performed at the famous Taormina Amphitheater several years earlier, and he wanted to bring her back, with my help. Her previous trio of shows had been disappointing because they had not been well publicized, and because three nights were too many for a large venue like the five thousand-seat Teatro Antico amphitheater in Taormina. He felt sure Liza would be a sellout under different circumstances.

I contacted her agent, who informed me that Liza was performing in Monaco and had some free days afterward. She would agree to a contract for a one-night show if we met her in Nice and escorted her by chartered plane to the Messina airport near Taormina.

I was told there should be no mini-bar in Liza's room—an unsettling piece of advice for any producer. We had one day to travel and prepare. Liza would perform the next evening. There was no rain date. When I met Liza with her entourage of about thirty at the Nice airport, she was wearing nondescript pants and a loose blouse, her face hidden by sunglasses and a baseball cap. No one recognized her. As she stepped out of the limo, she put her arm in mine, and I escorted her slowly to the gate. I knew that she had had hip and knee replacements, but I had not expected her to be quite as infirm. She could hardly walk. How would she be able to perform?

We boarded the small private plane I had arranged and took our seats.

Upon arrival, while the entourage waited for their bags, I whisked her off to Hotel San Domenico, so she could get some rest before that afternoon's press conference. Unfortunately, the interpreter was less than facile; her translations were so limited that I asked to take over. Liza was delighted, thanked me, and hugged me. Despite her bravado, she clung to my arm as we walked around the hotel. Her physical and emotional fragility were unnervingly evident.

The local promoter had arranged for an extravagant dinner on the rooftop of Ristorante Baronessa, which boasted a view of the moonlit Mediterranean to one side and the Taormina terraces to the other. It looked like a scene from *Lucia de Lammermoor*. Liza sent polite regrets, but the setting was magical, even without the star of the night—as were the *Lamuri vini* and the specially designed five-course seafood menu, beginning with *insalatina di gamberi* followed by *spaghetti chimera alla bottarga* and *spigola al forno*. The meal was as memorable as the setting.

The following day was cloudy, with only brief flashes of sun. We were all worried that we would be rained out, but ticket sales were brisk, despite the uncertain forecast. By late afternoon, we were sold out. Our good friends Maria Paola Martelli, Lietta Cavalli, and her husband, Francesco, had flown in from Florence for the weekend. I knew it would be a nightmare to enter through the front gate of the amphitheater with the public an hour before the performance. Fortunately, to avoid a big detour and commotion as thousands were arriving at the entrance gate to the amphitheater, I managed to convince the Timeo Hotel guard that I was the producer. He opened the grand wrought-iron gate, which led to a path through lush private *giardini*. The stroll up the path was an unexpected luxury: a chance to enjoy the tranquility of the surroundings before the evening's excitement.

When we reached the amphitheater, it was filling up nicely for the 9 p.m. show. To my great relief, the sky was clearing. It was a perfect, starlit evening. After making sure that Liza was happy and all her pre-performance requirements were met, I went to find my seat. I soon spotted our friends, who waved excitedly as I walked up the crowded aisle, drink in hand.

"*Come stai, Maria Paola. Tutto bene?*"

"*Si, carissimo. Siamo pronti per la diva!*"

I noted that the theater was completely filled, except for two rows in the front, equipped with what looked like oversized leather armchairs. They were incongruous, to say the least, in this ancient setting.

"What are these large chairs?" I asked in Italian. "Who sits in them?"

"*Sono i posti riservati per . . . persone importanti,*" Lietta informed me.

The seats remained empty during Liza's performance, but I imagined a number of *Padrini*—godfather figures—lounging comfortably in their enormous lounge chairs with their backs to the audience, unconcerned with their own safety, despite the vulnerability of this set-up.

The performance was delightful—due largely to the fact that Liza had a group of dancers to help her move around the stage. Knowing how much trouble she had walking, I was astonished that she could conceal her physical limitations so well. She still had a knockout powerful voice. Everyone was transfixed when she belted out "New York, New York," and charmed when she told them how much she had longed to return to Taormina. "I used to be able to stand for the entire show," she joked at one point, "but now I have to sit during the second half." This confession only further endeared her to the crowd. Then Liza told some stories about her childhood in New York City, including some with her godmother, singer-actor Kay Thompson, who is most famous for penning the iconic book *Eloise*, about a young child growing up in the penthouse of the Plaza Hotel. When my daughter Nadia was eight, I took her to the Plaza's Palm

Court, a restaurant immortalized in *Eloise*. Nadia asked where Eloise lived, and one of the staff took us up to the top floor to show us "Eloise's apartment." I'll never forget the wonder of that moment, experiencing it, as I did, through Nadia's eyes. Liza dedicated the night's performance to Thompson.

Sitting under the stars with a packed-to-capacity crowd, it felt like a night at the opera. After a standing ovation of many minutes, the concert ended, and we headed to a gala reception on the outdoor terrace of the Grand Hotel Timeo, where at night the view of the sea was magical. Liza arrived with her hairdresser, who was also her close friend and confidant. Phyllis and I were joined by several of our Italian friends. At one point, someone handed me a note saying that two diplomats, one Israeli and one German, were asking to be admitted to see Liza. I headed down a few steps to the stage door, and once outside, found an enormous crowd pressing against the protective railing. It was bedlam. The throngs of clamoring fans reminded me of the Segovia days a quarter-century earlier.

Not knowing how to identify the men, I opened the stage door and called out to the restless crowd: *"Ever tov"* ("Good evening" in Hebrew). Not surprisingly, the man who responded was the Israeli ambassador to the Holy See, Oded Benhur. I was very pleased to offer him an opportunity to meet Liza. The German ambassador was probably a fine gentleman, but—in perhaps not my finest moment—I couldn't resist making the slight. The wounds from WWII are still so raw for me that when Phyllis, Nadia, and Alexis visited Berlin a few years earlier, I had found myself unable to join them.

Liza was circumspect about her personal life, but she did share one poignant story. Phyllis, looking for a way to connect with her personally, mentioned that Leopold Godowsky had stayed with us in our home in Fiesole a few weeks earlier. Leopold is George Gershwin's nephew. Liza was named for a George Gershwin song by the same name, because her mother, Judy Garland, was very close to George and Ira. Liza recounted the following story:

Liza

George had begun to complain of headaches, but doctors, having little imaging technology at the time, could find nothing wrong with him and dismissed his complaints of exhaustion and depression as merely "ennui." His family seemed to accept the diagnosis of "psychosomatic" pain, and only when he began to behave oddly, had a brief seizure while performing, and became so weak he couldn't walk to the bathroom without support from his brother Ira, was he taken from his Beverly Hills home to the emergency room at Cedars of Lebanon in 1937. Surgeons then discovered a large glioblastoma in his brain, and although they worked for four hours to remove it, he died on the operating table. Liza told us that Judy was at Gershwin's Beverly Hills home that afternoon, waiting with the family by the phone. When the news came—that not only had George been suffering from a brain tumor, but that he had died in surgery—a shocked silence followed. Then, Frances, George's younger sister, who had been very close with him, abruptly stood up, announcing, "I think I'll make some eggs."

Phyllis and I became quite close with Leopold Godowsky, George's nephew, and one Yom Kippur, we invited him and Frances to a breakfast at our Riverside Drive apartment. Frances was then eighty-nine. The moment they walked in, she asked to use the restroom. We were concerned that something was wrong, but she quickly reappeared. "Just had to fix my hair!" she quipped. The winds on Riverside Drive are legendary, and Frankie was still very much the grand dame!

A year later, we met the Israeli ambassador, Oded Benhur, for lunch in Rome. He told us stories about his friendship with winemaker Franco Biondi Santi, a Brunello "saint" idolized by oenophiles. I was particularly touched by the meeting. I consider myself virtually Italian when I'm with my Italian friends, and my Jewishness fades, for me, into the background. To serendipitously meet an Israeli ambassador who was as comfortable in Italy as I was gave me a sense of cultural camaraderie I rarely get to experience. "Home" is an elusive concept for me, but to be able to identify with this man on *two* levels gave me an evanescent sense of "home." It also gave me an almost mystical sense of the hidden roots joining all the cultures of the world. I remember how comfortably we switched back and forth between Hebrew, Italian, and English, a blending of languages that never threatened their discrete essences—a metaphor, perhaps, for the sharing of the performing arts internationally. Over time, these languages may borrow from each other and thus evolve, but their distinctive roots remain. Lastly, it was pleasant to find camaraderie in a fellow ambassador—he represented Israel at the Holy See, and I was a cultural ambassador for my adopted country, America.

14

Tamara, a Playful Scherzo

*I*n 1987, a new play called *Tamara* opened at the Park Avenue Armory. Curious, I read about the show, discovering it was three hours long and included a grand buffet dinner catered by chef Daniel Boulud for all the guests at intermission. The cost of a ticket was $150, which included dinner, but it struck me as extravagant. Still, the play sounded interesting and was certainly innovative: the action sprawled over a dozen rooms and involved ten actors playing their parts as they moved from room to room, sometimes alone and sometimes interacting with other characters. Audience members could follow the character of their choice or switch among characters.

Although a number of productions use a similar formula today, at the time it was entirely new and quite daring. One day I received an unexpected call from my friend and colleague, Giovanni Soresi, head of the press office at Piccolo Teatro, in Milan, introducing me to *Contessa* Adriana Sterzi. She wanted to sponsor Tamara at D'Annunzio's palazzo on Lago di Garda, the setting of the play. (The palazzo is named "Il Vittoriale degli Italiani.") The Contessa flew to New York from Moscow in January of 1990, armed with several pounds of caviar, and invited Phyllis and me to dine at her *pièd-a-terre* overlooking the U.N. Her apartment was not large, but the table was set in grand style, with champagne and the lavish beluga caviar that shone like translucent pearls. The evening was an unexpected treat, but I doubted it would materialize into a real sponsorship, even if I could find a venue for *Tamara*, which I had not yet seen. How realistic was it to bring this highly sophisticated theater piece to Italy?

Moreover, the piece, created by John Krizanc, revolved around a real historical meeting between Art Deco painter Tamara de Lempicka and Italian writer-turned-war hero Gabriele D'Annunzio at his villa (Il Vittoriale degli Italiani) on Lago di Garda, where D'Annunzio was under house arrest by order of "Il Duce" (Benito Mussolini). The play portrayed him as a shameless womanizer intent on seducing de Lempicka.[1] Would the Italians be comfortable with a play that depicted D'Annunzio, a national icon and an idealized poet, whose work every Italian child reads, as a predator?

Despite my trepidation, the Contessa's enthusiasm was contagious, and so, with some reservations, I agreed to "reproduce" the Tamara experience for Italian audiences. We went to the Park Avenue Armory and were swept away by the staging, the Le Cirque dinner, and the political and personal intrigue of the play.

I began to research *Tamara* and discovered that the show had played to sold-out audiences for two years at the Armory. Many people returned again and again to follow different characters and have a new experience each time. *New York Times* critic Mel Gussow described it as an "entertaining party game and murder mystery theme park, unlike any other show currently in New York," and "a shot of adrenalin for sedentary theatergoers who are accustomed to sitting in the dark and watching actors do all the work."[2] After seeing it, I agreed.

And, so, I began the daunting task of mounting *Tamara* at two different villas in Italy. I was able to obtain the sponsorship of Omega, which saw an opportunity to promote their new watch, *Swatch*. Unfortunately,

Tamara, a Playful Scherzo

finding a villa that met the required criteria was no small feat. The Armory has three stories and plenty of staircases and space, making it an ideal venue for the sprawling and intricate production. It was hard to imagine replicating *Tamara* without an equivalently generous space. Giovanni came through again.

We needed a large living area where guests could gather, ideally with a grand staircase, and space and facilities to serve at least one hundred guests an elegant dinner. D'Annunzio's own palazzo was large enough but too packed with valuable collectibles to make it a viable performance venue. Ultimately, we settled on three weeks of performances at Villa Brasini in Rome, historically a gathering place for heads of state (both Mussolini and D'Annunzio dined there), followed by five weeks at Villa Erba, the Visconti villa next to Villa d'Este on Lake Como. One of the many complications of producing *Tamara* was that the script had to be extensively adjusted for every new venue; entrances, exits, and meetings among the characters had to be worked into the script according to the layout of the space. This meant that the playwright needed three weeks lead time after the new venue had been chosen to study it and make the necessary adjustments accordingly. It was an enormous jigsaw puzzle. Add to this the rehearsals and the prep time for the understudies, and it was a daunting project.

The cast was chosen by director George Rondo (1930–2013) from actors who had performed in *Tamara* in New York, and my dear friend Giovanni Soresi, of Piccolo Teatro in Milano, not only found the venue, but supplied the national press a detailed description of this unique spectacle. The press conference allowed me to indulge in a moment of vanity: I had finally become comfortable enough to sustain an interview in Italian. I started speaking in English, pausing a bit to allow journalists to translate, and then asked them, "*Volete continuare nella piu' bella lingua del mondo?*" ("Shall I continue in Italian?") And I did! After fifteen delightful years of work in *bella Italia*, I was quite at home with the language of Dante and Petrarca.

On opening night at Villa Brasini, Tamara de Lempicka's daughter, Kizette de Lempicka (1916–2001), flew in from Texas, and the grandson of Gabriele D'Annunzio (1943–1996), as eccentric as his grandfather, arrived on a white horse. The lavish catered meal was similar to those served by D'Annunzio himself and was presented in the style of 1927, with elaborate candelabra and artistically presented platters of *Insalata di Penne Profumate, Carciofi alla Barigoule,* and *Supremes di Sogliole alla d'Estre.* Italian wines flowed, including a Chardonnay Crémant, a Cabernet Franc and Pramaggiore DOCG.

Our daughters, then ages nine and six, attended the opening-night performance and were enthralled by the fairytale feeling of the whole affair. Not only could they stay up late, but they were in a grand villa, where an actual prince had arrived on an actual white horse! They moved comfortably through the villa with the other well-dressed guests, though Phyllis and I had to take care that they didn't wander into a room where the exchanges were too risqué. It wasn't easy, as Nadia was particularly intrigued by the relationship between D'Annunzio and de Lempicka. After dinner, the children were ushered to bed, much to their disappointment.

Tamara was a tour de force and a major success in Italy. Since D'Annunzio is a household word in Italy, the press and public were very responsive. On many evenings, the audience dressed in the fashion of the 1920s. The villa was filled with flappers wearing beaded headpieces and shimmering sequined dresses. The actors were almost lost among the guests. In fact, on opening night at Villa Erba, the sophisticated Milanese crowd was attired so fittingly for the occasion and so engaged with each other that some of the actors ended up feeling frustrated that they had lost control of the show! Enthralling as audiences found *Tamara*, actors found the show incredibly demanding. They were extremely close to the audience, and they were always competing with the other actors for attention. It was contractually specified that each actor had to perform every scene whether or not any audience members had followed them. If they didn't, it would disrupt the timing and flow of the other intersections and scenes. Inevitably, it behooved the

Tamara, a Playful Scherzo

actors to garner at least some audience, giving them the stress of enticing members to follow them by sheer charismatic pull. (More than once we had to admonish actors who directly addressed audience members, asking them to follow them to the next scene). Needless to say, the constant demands of the production from insecure actors to the logistics of movement throughout the Villas, caused me significant stress. This reached a crescendo on Lago de Como when I tripped on the grand staircase and sprained my ankle, requiring crutches for the remainder of the run.

After the success in Italy, hoping to produce *Tamara* in other countries, I saw many more performances in LA and New York, and I noticed, unsurprisingly, that I enjoyed it more as I became more familiar with the characters. Seeing it repeatedly was part of the appeal, because choosing to follow a different character gave you an entirely different experience! *The New York Times* calculated that there are many possible experiences of the play.[3] Doing *Tamara* at other venues was always enticing, but I faced two major problems: First, it was very hard to find an appropriate venue for an open-ended run. Second, it was a challenge to secure another sponsorship.

We came painfully close to an extended run at a villa in Kyoto, but this opportunity never materialized. It fell through at the last minute, because the wife of the owner of the Grand Supermarket chain was afraid the evening gatherings would cause too much commotion. She was worried that it would be disruptive to have guests coming and going every night near her high-rise apartment overlooking the Villa—even after my two trips to Kyoto and after the potential presenter had sent a contingent of twelve people to LA to be seduced by the *Tamara* experience.

Beginning in 1984, I had worked on many projects with Tokichi Takada, a Japanese promoter, a warm, affable man of vision who also became a true friend.

Not only did we share projects over the years, such as bringing *Porgy and Bess* to fifteen cities in Japan as well as to the two opera houses in Tokyo and *Broadway Tonite*, but he had invited me into his private world, which was very unusual for a Japanese man. On one trip, Tokichi took me to an authentic *ohnsen* in a rural part of Japan called Sendai. (An *ohnsen* is a hot spring and its associated bathing facilities.) It was after midnight, the air icy cold, as we undressed and submerged ourselves in the near-boiling spring. After a few minutes, the door to the bathing area opened, and to my great surprise, two women who were around the age of eighty entered. They were nude, chubby, covering only their pubic areas with small squares of cloth. They did not make eye contact with us, instead acknowledging our existence with a small kind of salute. They descended three steps into our hot spring and soaked for a time, undisturbed by our presence. Knowing about cultural differences is quite separate from actually experiencing them, and I found myself amazed by this tableau, as if an invisible curtain had descended between them and us. Nevertheless,

Tamara, a Playful Scherzo

there was the courteous bow when they departed. The Japanese are generally so modest that massage is usually performed over clothing. On the other hand, it was hard to accept Tokichi's misogynous behavior when he invited me to his country house near Mount Fuji and had his young niece cater to us the entire weekend.

After the success in Italy, my cousin Kitty tried to find us a venue in London. I visited her at her Mayfair house in the spring of 1997, and we went together to look at possible locations. Being well connected in the art world, Kitty also had some ideas for sponsors. With her enthusiastic backing, I was optimistic that I could launch *Tamara* in London.

Then something truly shocking happened. That December, just a few months later, a fire raged at Kitty's Upper East Side townhouse. She perished in the fire. I was in London at the time, staying at the Dukes Hotel, which Kitty had suggested. Nadia was with me for this second trip to tour venues. Nadia and I had an early-morning flight home the next day. I will never forget coming downstairs in the early-morning hours to check out. The hotel's lobby was small and dark, illuminated only by a lamp that was aimed like a spotlight on a stack of the December 19, 1997 *London Times* on the desk. There, on the front page, was Kitty's familiar face staring up at me. Below the large photo, the headline read: "Socialite dies rescuing friends."

Kitty was only sixty when she died, and a remarkable model of creativity and entrepreneurial success. She was also one of the first people who believed in me when I first arrived in New York. She had helped me secure my all-important, life-altering Green Card. Her loss has been mitigated only by her largesse, which lives on in vivid memories.

Larry Rivers, a good friend and prominent artist, played the saxophone at her funeral. Phyllis felt he described Kitty perfectly: "She was a social creature beyond belief. Her tables looked like Dutch still-life paintings—8,000 things on the table, oversized fish, oversized fruit, everything lavish. It was beautiful." She would have loved to design the D'Annunzio dinner. Indeed, her homes in Mayfair, in Southampton, her townhouse in Manhattan's East 60s were eclectic but always elegant—and as dramatic as a D'Annunzio villa.

After losing Kitty, I abandoned my efforts to launch *Tamara* in London. It wouldn't have been the same without her. In the years since, I've watched a number of productions adopt John Krizanc's formula to create such hits as *Dionysus in 69*, *Tina and Tony's Wedding*, and *Sleep No More*. *Tamara* was the progenitor for all of them.

I have attempted a revival in New York City several times, but despite great enthusiasm, it has proven a challenge to find an appropriate venue for a long-term run. Though Nadia was only nine when she saw *Tamara* in Italy, she still remembers the fun and excitement. In 2015, she convinced me to produce it again in New York. I tried and almost got a green light from The Downtown Association, a private club near Wall Street that would have been an ideal venue, but, at the last minute, they decided against it. Not long ago, I was approached by Marisa Loporto, a great granddaughter of de Lempicka, about producing the play in New York, and as I write this, I am still exploring the possibility.

15

Porgy and Me

*J*n the summer of 1991, I was asked to locate a production of *Porgy and Bess* for the opening of the fall season in Buenos Aires at the elite Teatro Colon. The Italian *nouveau riche* of Argentina had built the theater to compete with the grand opera houses of Italy, especially with the venerable La Scala, and indeed, it did. They replicated La Scala except for its size. Teatro Colon is *bigger*. La Scala has 2,030 seats; Teatro Colon has 2,487. La Scala has four loges; Teatro Colon has five.

Although I had launched the idea of the Houston Grand Opera tour in Italy in 1976, I knew that that production was too cumbersome for touring. Luckily, I found a new, highly acclaimed *and* less elaborately staged version of the Gershwin classic that had been mounted by the talented conductor Peter Mark at the Virginia Opera and was available to tour.

The Gershwin heirs, who hold the worldwide rights to *Porgy and Bess*, were not only receptive to the idea and royalty agreement but also eager to attend the opening night themselves at South America's premier opera house. I had not actually met them, because all the negotiations had been handled by their agent, Louis Aborn (1912–2005). Although I thought it was a significant gesture of approval that they were making the

153

trip to Buenos Aires, I thought it would be a one-time opportunity. The Virginia Opera production had little experience touring, but they were thrilled to have the opportunity to perform at Teatro Colon. I shared their excitement, partially because I had never been to Buenos Aires, a city I had heard was like mid-century Europe, and the opening night of the fall season (our spring season) was a big deal.

Shortly after the contracts were signed, my Japanese business partner and friend Tokichi Takada announced that he was coming to New York to celebrate his 60th birthday with me—at the exact time I needed to be in Argentina. I knew he would be disappointed if I were not available. Tokichi had become much more than a business contact. We had collaborated on multiple projects, starting in 1984 with *Broadway Tonite*, and then working on tours of The Spanish National Ballet with Maya Plisetskaia (1925–2015). Over time, Tokichi had begun to trust me, which I knew was rare. In my experience, Japanese men do not easily place their trust in outsiders.

Peter and Tokichi Takada

Porgy and Me

Not wanting to miss his birthday, I thought fast. Over the phone, I spontaneously invited him to join us in Buenos Aires for the premiere of *Porgy and Bess* at the Teatro Colon. I thought that he would decline—after all, it was a ten-hour flight! But to my surprise, he accepted immediately. Suddenly, I was consumed with worry: what if I couldn't give him the special attention I knew he would expect? Would I be able to mark his birthday as a special event in the midst of launching a major tour? A fancy meal with nice wine wouldn't cut it. I decided I had to give him an experience that was unusual, theatrical, and memorable. In other words, I felt compelled not only to celebrate his birthday, but to *produce* it.

He and Phyllis were on the same flight—arriving one night before the evening of the premiere. They didn't interact much, as Takada found conversation and friendship uncomfortable as a traditional Japanese man who spoke limited English. This was fine with Phyllis even though she was alone during a harrowing flight. Fog had twice delayed the plane's landing, and there was talk of a one hundred-mile diversion if the third attempt proved futile. Fortunately, however, the pilot was able to land the plane at B.A. Pistarini Airport, as planned. Tokichi seemed quite shaken, but I had little time to attend to him since I was immersed in the opening-night details at Teatro Colon, not to mention trying to decipher the nuances of Argentinian culture, the better to manage the usual backstage dramas.

The first part of the rehearsal went surprisingly well, so I was disturbed to see Marc Gershwin running up to me, clearly agitated. A thousand potential problems raced through my mind. Had there been some inadvertent breach of contract? Did he have a problem with a singer? The orchestra? Recently, he had requested that we replace *Bess* because he may have thought that her bosom was too ample. I had refused. She was a wonderful performer with a gorgeous voice, keenly capable of expressing the pathos of the role. I was surprised and relieved to hear that this time, Marc's complaint was personal. His seats, he told me, were in a Parterre box, not the Royal Box...

I was still uncertain that the very white Argentine audience would appreciate an opera that spoke to the tribulations and heartache of poverty in a Black community. In the 1990s, Argentina still harbored plenty of racist attitudes and conservative ways of thinking.

Additionally, opening night of the fall season meant an audience filled with politicians and other culturally influential people. I was counting on Gershwin's melodic, haunting score to entrance theatregoers, but audience reactions are famously hard to predict. It was a delicate balance; a show should feel new and exciting, but not too avant-garde, or we risked losing the audience.

To my delight and enormous relief, the production was a big success on opening night at the Teatro Colon on April 7, 1992. The press praised the cast—the same one that performed in Norfolk, plus an expanded chorus of thirty-four members—as "a highly professional group of people that understands the work, has a feeling for the score and commands it in depth."[1] Critic Emilio Giminez called it "an exemplary version" of the opera. *"Brillante!"* announced *La Nacion*. *"Excepcional!"* raved the *Clarin*.

But my worries were not behind me. I was still fretting about Tokichi Takada's sixtieth-birthday celebration, and, at the same time, I needed to accommodate the Gershwins' expectations for introductions and dinners.

I had the idea of arranging a fireworks extravaganza that would display "TT60" in the sky. Six years earlier, to mark the opening of the Consulate General of Italy in Houston, I had coordinated a fireworks extravaganza with my dear friends Monica Maimone, Valerio Festi, and Luca Brofferio, the Italian consul general. It is engraved in my memory. Creative fireworks leaped out as a perfect gift for Tokichi. How could I find a setting for such a presentation? My colleague Elias Grappa, who was instrumental in arranging the *Porgy and Bess* tour, put me in touch with a fireworks company.

I learned that fireworks displays weren't allowed at downtown restaurants, but only on the outskirts of Buenos Aires, on Rio de la Plata. This was no small challenge, particularly for a stranger in Buenos Aires.

Porgy and Me

Worse, I had to plan a dinner to honor Tokichi, but I was hosting the Gershwin heirs for the first time, and I would be compromising on the quality of the meal in favor of a restaurant whose neighborhood allowed for the elaborate presentation I was planning. Since this was not a first-class restaurant, I was concerned that the Gershwins might feel slighted but was pleased that they were accommodating.

The night after the opening, I invited the Gershwins and Tokichi to dinner. Thanks to the local red wine, we were all so tipsy we could hardly stand up. A few minutes before 10 p.m., when the fireworks were scheduled to go off, I planned to have everyone go outside. When I suggested we get some fresh air, Tokichi resisted. "I am not interested," he said. I had to coax him and enlist help from the others, who knew about the surprise. Eventually, he consented, and all nine of us made our way outdoors. At exactly 10 p.m., the lights went off, there was a moment of silence, and then: *Bang!* This formal, constrained Japanese gentleman was visibly overcome with surprise and delight when "TT 60" appeared across the misty moonlit sky.

The Gershwins also enjoyed the surprise spectacle. The group included Marc Gershwin, son of Arthur Gershwin (brother of George and Ira), Leopold Gershwin Godowsky (son of George's sister Frances), Mike Strunsky (nephew of Ira), and their spouses. At the time, I didn't think of future business with them. I thought it would be difficult to tour an opera with a cast and orchestra this size, and I doubted it would have widespread appeal while more commercial Broadway musicals—with smaller casts and orchestras—were extensively touring coast to coast. However, I did ask the Gershwins if they would consider a national tour after the enthusiastic response in Buenos Aires, to which they gave immediate approval.

After getting their consent, I called my booker and asked him to reach out to twenty theaters across the country to see if there would be interest in a touring production. I assumed the odds were slim, because the major cities had probably seen the Houston Grand Opera production's uncut version, which had been received with mixed reviews. Instead, they *all* responded positively and mentioned a few *additional* theaters that wanted to be included in a potential tour. Now I felt I had a winner. It was a good thing I didn't realize then the scope of what I was taking on, because if I had, I might have passed.

In retrospect, a *Porgy and Bess* tour was well-timed: white audiences were belatedly becoming interested in the experiences of Black Americans. Also, Gershwin's score was familiar to many of them, particularly the songs "Summertime" and "It Ain't Necessarily So," having entered popular culture as frequently played jazz standards. I asked the Gershwin heirs if they would license a production specifically for touring, meaning less-elaborate sets and smaller venues. They responded enthusiastically. I liked to think that the strange and magical night we shared due to the chance confluence of a good friend's birthday and an Argentinean premiere had resonated and increased their faith in me.

Once the Gershwins gave me the go-ahead, I sought a top-notch director. Leopold Godowsky suggested I speak to Arvin Brown, who had just mounted a successful production of *Porgy* at the New York Metropolitan Opera. I hadn't seen it, but the reviews had been mixed. Some criticized the long production as unimaginative and "overblown," and I heard that a good part of the audience *went on their* way before . . . Porgy was on *his* "way to the Promised Land," as he sings in his closing aria. I needed someone with a new vision.

Shortly after *Porgy's* 1992 Teatro Colon premiere, Leopold invited me to see a production at the Civic Light Opera in Pittsburgh, directed by Will Roberson (1958–1994). I really liked it and began to consider Will as a director for my new production. I asked him to propose a fresh version of *Porgy*. Within half an hour, I was sold. First, he envisioned a very different set. Almost all previous productions depicted Catfish Row as a series of dilapidated brownstone buildings with windows and narrow staircases, allowing little space for the cast to move around the stage. Will devised a simple but suggestive set on three levels that created an open stage, enhancing movement and allowing the action to soar. For the opening of the second scene, set on Kiawah Island, Will created an intimate corner for Serina's "My Man's Gone Now," using dramatic lighting effects to evoke the sunset.[1]

The Gershwins allowed us to make very substantial cuts to the production, in order to make touring a realistic possibility. This brought the show down to less than three hours. The Met's production had been more than four and a half.

My bright, dedicated, and talented administrator, Diana Geffner Ventura, helped to bring the production to life. We chose to kick off the tour in Charleston, South Carolina, home of the real Catfish Row, with Kiawah Island nearby. We opened on January 15, 1993 to smashing reviews in the *Post and Courier*, the local paper. A few days later, we played to sold-out houses two nights in a row in Greenville, South Carolina. I even spotted two ads in the local paper from people seeking tickets!

Backstage, it was another story. By now, I had extensive touring experience with theatrical and dance groups, but I was unprepared for these particular challenges. After the Charleston opening and the exceptional reviews, the cast was exhilarated. But by the time we reached Greenville, their mood had changed. They began demanding higher-quality hotels, higher per diems, shorter travel times, and other terms that went beyond their contracts.

I was exhausted and drained from getting us to opening night, and now, instead of enjoying our success, I felt bombarded by complaints. I even got calls in my room.

"The breakfast was really skimpy."

"There was no place to eat after the performance."

"The bus ride was too long."

"We're being underpaid."

Politically and emotionally, it was a complex situation. I was the White producer at the helm of an all-Black cast and, due to the blatant racism of the labor unions, an all-White crew and orchestra. Hoping to avoid friction on the road and wanting as integrated a company as possible, I had tried to find Black crew and orchestra members. I hadn't had success. I had asked Kevin Jeff, our Black choreographer, to help me find Black candidates for other roles such as stagehands, lighting and sound technicians, and wardrobe mistress, only to learn that the Italian/Irish labor unions weren't open to Black membership. In essence, they were private clubs handing down membership from generation to generation—another kind of Mafia.

Phyllis, my in-house psychological consultant, helped me to grasp the complex dynamics at play (and the importance of setting limits). She gave me some much-needed perspective. Many of these accomplished singers worked alternate jobs as taxi drivers and schoolteachers to survive between productions. Their demands were deep-rooted in a profound lack of trust that stemmed from living within a chronically racist society all their lives. Not surprising, they were deeply suspicious. For example, some complained that the hotel accommodations were subpar, even though most of the hotels were three-star. I tried very hard to establish trust by riding the same bus and by listening to their opinions on whom in the cast and crew were team players and who might need to be replaced. Over the years, as the company toured together consistently, we all did settle into a kind of family.

Unfortunately, our box office success did not translate into an immediate windfall, largely because touring with a thirty-five-piece orchestra was extremely expensive. After the 1993 tour, I asked Leopold, a musician and composer himself who made the artistic decisions for Gershwin material, to approve the idea of reducing the score. He did, on the condition that we use Steve Cohen, a professional orchestrator.

I contacted Cohen, who turned out to be a reasonable and talented professional. He reduced three five-minute excerpts from the score, including "It Ain't Necessarily So," "Summertime," and "Bess, You Is My Woman Now" in a few weeks.

The Gershwins also insisted I book a concert hall and hire eighteen musicians for a trial of the revised score. I chose the lovely, wood-paneled main auditorium of the 92nd Street Y. It was a sunny Sunday afternoon, and the musicians had practiced the new score for several hours before we arrived. Nonetheless, I was very anxious. I had invested so much in the effort for it all to come to nothing now. It was just too financially impractical to continue to tour with the original-size orchestra.

As the Gershwins and some guests they'd invited arrived, Phyllis and I were perched in our chairs like nervous swallows, watching the scene unfold. Next to us were Leopold and his wife, Elaine. David Stahl (1949–2010) began to conduct the first number, "It Ain't Necessarily So." Midway through the piece, Leopold got up and walked onto the stage; he seemed to be agitated. He asked David to step aside. I began to sweat ice cubes. Elaine was so nervous that she grabbed Phyllis's hand.

Leopold then took Stahl's baton and began conducting the eighteen musicians himself! "This is an astonishing act for Leopold," Elaine whispered. After this brief performance, Leopold handed the baton back to Stahl, walked back to his seat, and smiled broadly.

"Kudos. Accepted," he said.

Still, I couldn't relax completely until I had the contract in hand. I was delighted when I got written confirmation from Louis Aborn, the Gershwin heirs' agent, that I could start booking the next tour with the reduced orchestra. Many weeks later, I learned that Leopold had seen the change as a tremendous risk. He worried that the reduced orchestra would reduce the impact of the gorgeous score and that the quality of the whole production would suffer as a result.

Several weeks later, Leopold and Elaine invited us for an afternoon of Lieder at their country house in Connecticut. Leopold cleared his throat and spoke before the assembled guests. "We are here because of Peter," he said. "Peter's courage in mounting the first-ever touring production of *Porgy and Bess* has encouraged me to come out of my seclusion and play the piano in public today, for the first time in 15 years. Thank you, Peter!" I was deeply moved.

To our surprise, his new outlook inspired him to leave the tranquility of Connecticut and move to an apartment in midtown Manhattan, just across from MOMA. He outfitted the apartment as a professional-grade recording studio. Leopold was now ready to compete in the big leagues. Our deep friendship lasted for the rest of his life.[2]

In 2002, we reduced the orchestra even further—increasingly sophisticated technology made it possible to produce much of the sound electronically. Today, many orchestras and "bands" for musicals use only five to seven musicians.

We intended to tour our streamlined production of *Porgy and Bess* for 2, maybe 3 seasons. Instead, it toured for 24 seasons, with more than 1,200 performances in 49 states, 25 countries on 6 continents.

In December of 1994, less than 2 years after our production launched, Will Roberson died of AIDS at only 36 years old. Not only did I miss him terribly, I worried that without Will, the production's quality would decline. My crew and I resolved to do our best to maintain the high level of our production without him.[3]

While on tour in 1997, Stephen Finch, one of my Porgys, met Susan Williams, a lovely Maori woman, in a bar in Christchurch, New Zealand. Not long after, they married. Susan, who had some experience in theater, asked to join the tour. I created a job for her in the wardrobe department. Bright, ambitious, and talented, she soon took over the wardrobe department. In a short time, I promoted her to stage manager. Not only was she highly organized and attuned to the cast's needs, but she created a positive *esprit de corps* on tour. She suggested subtle-but-significant modifications to the staging that improved the production immensely. By the time we returned to her native New Zealand in 2006, she had become our production manager. It was also my good fortune to have Jennifer Hoyt as our managing director. Jen, a seasoned opera singer, used her vast musical knowledge and experience to audition and add outstanding singers to the cast, while Susan maintained the quality of the staging.

I could also rely on Susan to resolve dissension among the performers and, if she couldn't, to let me know when it was necessary for me to intervene. It was critical that the cast work as a whole. Consistent troublemakers had to modify their behavior, or they'd be asked to leave. It was always very painful for me to let a performer go. It was my good fortune to have Dr. Elizabeth Graham as our principal Bess and stage director for several hundred performances. Her presence, professionalism, and style not only commanded respect but contributed to the *esprit de corps* of the company.

Despite our losing Will and the many difficulties of establishing and maintaining a cohesive company, I remained invested in a long run for *Porgy and Bess*, not just in the U.S., but worldwide. Excitement about the American dance scene had reached a fever pitch in the '70s and '80s, but now the hunger for everything American had expanded to include blue jeans, jazz, and, of course, our American opera, *Porgy and Bess*, although American jazz had been embraced since mid-century Paris.[4]

Working closely with so many Black performers taught me a great deal. I had worked with Black dance and theatrical companies before, ranging from Alvin Ailey, to Dance Theater of Harlem, from *Bubbling Brown Sugar* to *Ain't Misbehavin'*, but being engaged in the process of production from auditions onward with *Porgy* created an intimacy and special connection with the cast.[5]

16
Black and White

"When the actor Sidney Poitier agreed to star in the movie version of Porgy and Bess in 1959, he got a call from Harry Belafonte. "Man, don't do this work," Belafonte said. "This is not going to help our cause, some guy on his knees. Don't do it."
—AUSTRALIAN MAGAZINE, APRIL 19–20, 1997,
PG. 26, COSIC MIIRIAM

Porgy and Bess was the first great American opera, a fact the American public seemed a bit blind to at first. It was too accessible for opera, its hybrid of jazz and "serious" music too unlikely, and its story about poor Black Americans in a place called "Catfish Row"? Well!
—LLOYD DYKK, VANCOUVER SUN,
NOV. 18, 1993

When I first arrived in New York City in 1968, I perceived myself as the ultimate outsider. I'd walk down Broadway, mesmerized by the neon lights, the cacophony of sounds, the motion and swirl of passersby, and the varied and colorful styles of dress. My primary—perhaps only—concern as a young immigrant was making my mark on this vibrant culture. As a function of the era—not to mention my youth and naïveté—I was unaware of the vastness of racism and discrimination in America. In fact, I had idealized America. For me, this truly was the land of opportunity! The concept of white privilege was totally foreign. As a wide-eyed 23-year-old arriving here in the late 1960s, I had no such frame of reference. My naïveté was reinforced by the chance encounter that seemed to almost magically open the door to my theatrical career.

In the meantime, the civil rights movement that flowered in the 1950s and '60s had made a dent, but not enough of substance had been achieved to allay the deep-seated fear and trauma of Black America—as Harry Belafonte's plea above makes clear. Not only were there all the major concerns: voting rights, police brutality, and all the other savage inequalities woven into the fabric of the nation, there was the issue of identity and pride. How a Black person or any aspect of Black culture or history was depicted on a Broadway—or any other—stage was a highly sensitive issue for anyone invested in advancing the cause of equality in American Civil Rights. Not only that, White audiences had very limited interest in seeing theatre that expressed the culture or experiences of non-White people. But by the 1980s, there had been enough shift that an opera about Black people could actually bring in enough audience to financially sustain it.

When I began my backstage work with the performers represented by the Hurok office, I was immediately attracted to styles that were, culturally speaking, entirely unfamiliar to me. At the Masters Festival, which was my first time out as a producer, I presented The Rod Rodgers Dance Company, founded in 1966 to celebrate the Black-American experience and to highlight not just "the struggle for freedom and social change but also struggles to create innovative works."[1]

The performers were vibrant and what was fresh to my European eyes—their style of movement, their rhythm and way of being in the world—was what compelled me to put them on stage.

Black and White

Why did I choose to present Ambakaila, a Trinidadian folklore company and Black Caribbean group, for my first Italian tour? I never considered my choice as related to my past, but, as I look back, there is clearly a theme, a connection. Trinidad is intriguing because it is a multicultural melting pot with about a third of the population originating from Africa, a third from India, and the rest of mixed race. Perhaps I was captivated by this mix, which is expressed in the country's art and music. In fact, Phyllis was so intrigued by the multiplicity of Trinidad that she wanted to produce a documentary about it. Aubrey Adams, my Ambakaila contact, thought it was a great idea and even arranged a meeting for her with the Perle Mesta of Trinidad and the Trinidadian Minister of Culture.

In April 1977, upon arrival in Trinidad, Phyllis jauntily hailed a cab and was whisked off to a majestic sea-cliff villa with a grand veranda, in which she was cordially greeted by elite government officials and the minister of culture, who had been invited to hear her presentation. She pitched her idea with bold enthusiasm and then waited through an interminable pause. When they at last spoke, they pointedly questioned Phyllis's credentials to tell the stories of the people of Trinidad, not only people from another country, but people who were largely Black or Indian, and certainly not White. Phyllis laughs about her faux pas to this day, but again, it reflects how much more ignorant White Americans were then about overstepping our bounds and appropriating other cultures for our own uses. That meeting, however, certainly taught both of us a great deal.

When it comes to *Porgy and Bess,* many Black Americans and critics have responded similarly to a non-Black composer telling a story of Black-American experiences. "What has always been missing from George Gershwin's opera is what the situation of Porgy and Bess says about the *White* world. It is because of this omission that Americans are so proud of the opera. It assuages their guilt about Negroes, and it attacks none of their fantasies."[2]

Still, it is worth noting that Gershwin positioned the one white character—the detective (performed magnificently by our Master Detective Steve Simring and his very talented student Joseph Cahalan on my tours)—as a menacing intruder who arrives at the doorstep, gun in hand, in time to disrupt a sacred and intimate domestic ritual—a funeral. Even the score is interrupted when he appears, and the music does not resume until he leaves the stage. It does not seem a stretch to see this disruption of the melody as Gershwin's expressing his objection to the oppressive dominance of White America and his sympathy with Black America and its struggle to be free of it. (Simring put his own menacing twist on the character, choosing to pull out, instead of a gun, a toothpick, and proceed to clean his teeth in an expression of crassness and vulgarity in addition to leering dominance.)[3]

In 2011, at the initiative of my friend and colleague Agnes Havas, a Hungarian producer and impresario, I brought the American Classic *Ain't Misbehavin'*, presented in Europe as *Harlem Swing*, to a wildly successful engagement in Budapest. Sadly, with the current right wing regime of Victor Orban, with significant anti-immigrant fervor, I'm not confident how well it would be received now. I feel certain that my experience with Dr. Joseph Cuthbert on the Tobago tennis court was another *red wheelbarrow*—a pivotal moment in my life. I had met this man only once, but he trusted me enough to offer airfare for my Ambakaila tour. Maybe I wanted to return the unexpected and meaningful gift by providing new stages and audiences for Black performers. The pain of growing up a Jew in Eastern Orthodox Romania had never left me, and while I don't equate that hardship with the violence modern Black Americans have experienced here, it certainly predisposed me to promote their artists.

The exclusion of Blacks resonated because I too had longed for these things when I was marginalized for being a Jew among Catholics, a son of Capitalists among Communists, a Hungarian among Romanians. Although the first time I saw a Black person was at a Youth Communist Festival in Timișoara when I was sixteen, I had no close contact with Black

Black and White

people and culture until I arrived in the United States at twenty-three. I had much to learn about the degree of oppression here, the lack of integration, the systemic racism. It often struck me as ironic that White people flocked to Harlem to hear jazz; this, of course, betrayed my ignorance

of the racism's complexities. Our society happily chooses idols from a marginalized group while continuing to oppress that group as a whole. Enjoying Black musicians, even attending their shows, is certainly not an indication of being progressive. Meanwhile, it is incredible to think that the State Department touted *Porgy and Bess* as America's finest opera, touring the show worldwide all through the Cold War, while the country itself continued to be violently discriminatory and oppressive. In 1936, *Porgy and Bess* toured five cities during a two-month period, but—astonishingly—Black theatergoers were *not allowed in the Washington National Theater*. The cast refused to perform until the restriction was lifted, and eventually, the audience was integrated for these performances. The theater however did not officially change its policy until two decades later, in the 1950s.[4]

After my work with Dance Theater of Harlem in 1980–1981, educator and choreographer Marie Brooks (1929–2013) invited me to visit her Brooklyn dance school to consider the possibility of arranging a tour for her young, pre-professional dance group. I didn't know Brooklyn well and immediately got lost as I looked for the school—this was, obviously, long before the days of smartphones and GPS. But at last, I found it and discovered it had a fair-sized performance space on its ground floor. I hoped my visit wouldn't provide false hope to a group of teenagers whom I might ultimately decide were too green to tour internationally.

My concerns vanished within the first few minutes of watching these dedicated youngsters perform. Marie was obviously a passionate and gifted choreographer. Ultimately, I was very moved by their performance and determined to secure a tour for the group, which was called the Marie Brooks Pan African Dance Company. What especially persuaded me to undertake the project was Marie's crusade to educate and encourage Black children—and that the African-American community had embraced her as a hero for giving their children a unique opportunity.

I was confident that my cutting edge reputation combined with the Italians' love of children would secure a tour. I was right! They were a

Black and White

big hit— so much so that they were invited back for the next year! On a personal note, it was extremely gratifying to see these kids experience the beauty of Italy for the first time; it reminded me of my own first encounter with the wonders of this seductively beautiful and soul-satisfying country.

At about the same time, breakdancing was evolving in the streets of New York. A colleague suggested a group he had seen perform in Harlem. I was stunned by their clean technique and startling acrobatics, and I believed that touring them was a great idea. Spoleto audiences would undoubtedly thrill to the group's vibrant, explosive kinetic energy. It was authentic American dancing, birthed and developed on our urban streets. By now, I was also enjoying Gian Carlo Menotti's trust, having delivered several gems that had taken off with audiences at Spoleto in years past. He agreed to my new suggestion, because Maestro Menotti felt certain that I had my finger on the pulse of the Italian festival audience, their tastes and interests.

The troupe was excited about the prospect and prepared a live demo for me right on the city sidewalk. I loved it and offered them the tour, but the leader of the group was understandably wary about going to Italy—a place that, to them, seemed as remote as the moon. Finally though, he agreed. My office had to spend a good deal of time helping the dancers obtain their passports, and I made sure that the group—which I dubbed *The New York Express*—had a chaperone at all times once we arrived in Italy. I was not entirely certain that these young kids were going to be mature enough to handle an international tour, but my concern proved unfounded. They behaved like seasoned professionals, and once they took the stage, the love between them and the audience flowed strongly both ways.

It was personally very gratifying for me to be able to offer these green performers, whose experience of the world had been so limited, the thrill and adventure of performing on an international stage. In those days before the internet and cell phones, other countries felt much more like distant lands than they do today. In 1976, when I was paged poolside in the hotel in Tobago, that was an unusual thing—*a big deal*. Providing the foundation and the real experience of a successful international tour for these breakdancers was part of the reworking of my own early life, when it was hard to believe that any opportunity would arise.

In 1987, I met Vy Higginsen and Ken Wydro on an elevator in the Fenice Hotel in Venice. They were presenting *Mama, I Want to Sing!* at the New York in Venice festival, their musical about the African-American singer Doris Troy. (I was presenting *The Fantasticks* at the same festival.) Vy and Ken were with their nine-year-old daughter Knoelle, who was the same age as our older daughter and reminded me of how much I missed my family back home in New York. We struck up a conversation and, before long, became friends. In 1989, with an eye toward touring the show myself, I took Phyllis to a theater on upper Fifth Avenue to see it performed. I ended up presenting the show for years.[5] A few years later, talented Knoelle was an understudy in *Porgy and Bess* in the role of Clara.

My friend and Portuguese partner, Paulo Dias, was fascinated by the Black-American experience, so when I presented *Opera Nationale Italiana* ONI in Lisbon in 2001, I suggested presenting the *Harlem Gospel Choir* in Lisbon the following year. The culture there was still rather conservative, and the middle-aged audience arrived at the theater in business suits and ties for men and mid-century dresses for women, styles that would have been deemed old-fashioned by American standards. But the audience was so energized by the performance that, before long, they were dancing in the aisles. I was unprepared for this spontaneous eruption of joy and enthusiasm, and was extremely moved by it. The usually restrained audience connected easily with the performers, something I had not seen happen in the United States, where again, gospel is associated with Black Pentecostal churches—a culture that White America deems decidedly "other." The Portuguese had no such associations with the music, which freed them from that undermining prejudice, and allowed them to fully enjoy and appreciate what was happening on stage.

Black and White

Interestingly, in the early 1990s, when I was first touring *Porgy*, Black theatregoers often rejected it because they didn't like the way the show depicted Black America. It was too easy for White America to fold all of Black America into a stereotype of a struggling, poverty-stricken, violent, drug-addled community at the margins of society. I had seen the show as entirely respectful and utterly haunting in its beauty and pathos. It was easy for me, of course, as a European, to simply enjoy the music, to revel in its pathos, its haunting melodies, its vivid narrative. I could watch with no anxiety about how it would affect or reinforce perceptions of who I was.

The dynamic of a White producer at the helm of a Black cast was—to say the least—a complex one. I never wanted any performer to feel taken advantage of or used in a setting that could slow or deter social and civil progress. Where do the arts fit into such calculations? Certainly, no actor from a minority group wants to contribute to harmful stereotypes, but every performer wants to play major and challenging roles that provide fulfillment and greater exposure. How do we thread that needle? It is an imperfect process, bound to be riddled with wrong steps, miscalculations, and at times, great mistrust from those most vulnerable to being damaged by the process.

Not surprisingly, some performers may have thought I was out to take advantage of them. Despite my successes, I still had pangs of uncertainty and often considered myself so similar to these artists that I found it incredible they wouldn't trust me. After all, I was an immigrant and a foreigner and had struggled to be accepted myself. Only now, when I reflect upon my relationship with these artists and how distinctly different their experience was from mine, can I acknowledge the crushing impact racism has had on all areas of Black-American life. I may have had an accent, but it was not perceived as an indication of coming from a lower class. It is still the exception for White Americans *not* to judge Black linguistic heritage as inferior, something that must be corrected.

Given the historical oppression of Black Americans, it is ironic that many consider *Porgy and Bess* to be the quintessential American opera.

It is noteworthy that not only did George spend considerable time with the Gullah Black community in Charleston, but he was rumored to have had a love affair with Anne Brown, the first Bess. His nephew Leopold told Phyllis and me that Gershwin had changed the name of the opera from *Porgy* (the original title of the Heyward book), to *Porgy and Bess* because of Anne's emotional significance to him.

On another note, there has been much debate about the degree to which Gershwin—and his Jewish Tin Pan Alley contemporaries—were influenced by their cultural roots when composing the songs that would form The Great American Songbook. Gail Blache-Gill, a singer and professor of music from Trinidad who played many lead roles in my productions of *Porgy*, told me that when she heard the melody of "Baruch Atah Adonai" when she was in a synagogue to perform one day, she was struck by its similarity to "It Ain't Necessarily So," one of the many songs from *Porgy* that became a jazz standard. But musicologist Charles Hersch writes that "musical connections between Gershwin's music and "Jewish music" are slight.

It seems that for every expert who hears a connection, another dismisses it, and the controversy continues. Even a nine-record set of Dvorak's *New World Symphony*, which I heard frequently as a child, has a complex legacy for artists of color.[6]

Meanwhile, Gershwin did express an affinity for early Black-American music, stating: "I feel close to Negro music. In Russia, the country of my ancestors, folk music always finds a response." Given the debate over whether *Porgy* was an expression of cultural affinity or appropriation, the statement is certainly relevant. Perhaps even more relevant is what Todd Duncan, the first actor to portray the character of Porgy, expressed. Duncan said that the first time he heard the music, he "literally wept for what this Jew was able to express for the Negro."[7]

Looking back, I think that my producing *Porgy* was the culmination of decades of working with Black performers. It had not been the *only* focus of my work, but in retrospect, the number of projects I did with

Black and White

Black artists and groups was not a coincidence. It was also very meaningful to me that, over time, we saw Black theatregoers making up larger percentages of our *Porgy* audiences. When we first toured the show, Black theatergoers were, as I've stated, wary of a show that presented Black people as belonging to a permanent oppressed underclass, but as gains were made in terms of representation and equality, perhaps people could perceive the show as of a certain time and place, as about a *certain* group of Black people in the *past*, and not reflective of the current day. They could engage with the show on its artistic merits without perceiving it as an insult.

Throughout the years, I have been truly humbled by the strength and talent of artists like Arthur Mitchell, Marie Brooks, Bill T. Jones, and Alvin Ailey, whose visions have challenged American norms and allowed them to rise above the forces that would seek to oppress or minimize them. In the meantime, the brutality of this country continues but with, hopefully, more restraint and awareness.

17
Building Bridges

I toured *Porgy* in Australia and New Zealand in 1997 and again in 2006, both times for ten to twelve weeks. We hit all the major cities—and some smaller ones as well—in these two wonderful countries. Interestingly, I was able to import my production of *Porgy and Bess* to Australia only because they didn't have any Black opera singers. In exchange, I was required to host an Aborigine opera singer named Deborah Cheetham to New York for two months and provide master classes for her. I recently heard from Juno Gemes, a prominent Australian photographer, that she is having a very successful career.

Working in both these countries was wonderful. The tours ran smoothly since both sides' expectations were in sync. When issues arose, they were easily resolved because our cultures and language are similar. They appreciated the fact that we went through the trouble to bring this Gershwin masterpiece all the way from America. The same cannot be said of other countries we toured. The drama we encountered in Cairo, for example, was an opera in itself.

Cairo, April 2000

Our tour in Cairo started with a whim. One day, I contacted the cultural attache at Cairo's American Embassy about the possibility of a *Porgy and Bess* engagement. Much to my surprise, the office of Daniel C. Kurtzer, the American ambassador, responded enthusiastically. The Cairo opera house had burned down in the 1970s but had been rebuilt in 1988, thanks to a gift of $30 million from Japan to President Mubarak. Kurtzer's office put me in touch with the Egyptian Ministry of Culture to finalize the contract. In October of 1999, the foreign ministry sent me an 18-page document in English and Arabic with four signatures, a seal, and a technical rider for a Jan. 15, 2000 opening. The tour seemed to be falling into place, all the details addressed. Then, one morning in early December, I got a call from Ibrahim, my Egyptian contact at the Ministry of Culture. He informed me that they would have to postpone the engagement for "political reasons."

"But we have a contract," I protested.

"You may have a contract with four signatures and a seal, but it's not valid," Ibrahim informed me. "The fifth signature, the essential one, is missing."

I was beside myself with frustration. Had he deliberately sent me an invalid contract? Or was the contract, in fact, valid the way it was, and he was simply dissembling so that he could wiggle out of the contract for some mysterious reason? Either way, he was being thoroughly dishonest and deceptive—that much I knew. I also knew that the rules for doing business were different in Middle Eastern cultures. Even so, nothing could have prepared me for what followed.

I had already made commitments to the cast, musicians, and crew, so I wasn't willing to let the possibility of the tour die. I immediately phoned the American Embassy. "So sorry," was their response. "You're dealing with Egyptians. Different rules, different ethics, different morals. Ibrahim was lying to you. His superiors were probably doing the same to him."

Building Bridges

A short time later, I found out the truth from the American embassy: The move had nothing to do with politics. The Cultural Ministry had exceeded their budget with the Millennium celebrations held at the pyramids.

I suspect the American embassy put pressure on them, because a week later, Ibrahim called me to reschedule the engagement for April of 2000. When I told some of my friends and contacts in the arts world about my upcoming Cairo project, I was warned that different rules applied in this part of the world.

"You won't believe what happened when we were there six months ago," the administrator of the Joffrey Ballet told me. "We had to rent sound and light. We thought it was odd that this grand opera house with a state-of-the-art stage wouldn't have its own sound and light equipment." To their shock and dismay, my friends at the Joffrey found out that sound and light had indeed been part of the original gift from Japan, but the stagehands entrusted with maintaining it had removed the equipment little by little, so that visiting companies would have no choice but to rent it out . . . from them!

I thanked him for the information and made sure that equipment was included in my contract. Whew! I had avoided another trap.

Most of the fee for the new April dates was raised by the embassy. The Egyptian government had to contribute only $50,000. I requested that, one month prior to opening, they wire their portion to me. "Sorry," came the answer. "It's government money. We won't be able to do that."

"OK, please leave it with the American embassy," I suggested, knowing that was a source we both trusted.

"Sorry—we can't do that, either."

Ultimately, Ibrahim proposed that he meet us when we landed in Cairo and hand us the money right there at the airport. Needless to say, I was skeptical about this arrangement, but my hands were tied. I had already contracted with the entire cast and orchestra. People might have refused other opportunities in order to take part in this tour. I had also booked the airline tickets. I would compromise my reputation and lose credibility with my cast were I to withdraw now. *At least the embassy is involved*, I thought, trying to reassure myself. I had little choice but to hope for the best and trust Ibrahim to honor his promise.

We arrived at Cairo International Airport two days before opening night. Was Ibrahim there? Of course not. I could contact him only through his cell phone, and that was—surprise, surprise—out of service. At least the buses were there to pick us up and escort us to the hotel. A friend of mine and the actor portraying the role of the detective, Steve Simring, had come to Egypt with us, and we went from one *narghila* bar to another, explored the *souk*, and prepared for opening night.

We were informed that, at noon on the day of the premiere, there would be a press conference attended by the mayor of Cairo, the American ambassador, and other officials. Hearing this, I hit upon a plan to force Ibrahim's hand and collect my missing $50,000.

Shortly after noon, everyone arrived. I then asked my conductor and lead singers to join me outside the entrance to the conference room. The press conference couldn't start without us.

A scrawny, agitated little man I had never seen before appeared.

"Mr. Peter, Mr. Peter! Let's start the conference," he said nervously. "The press is waiting!"

"Who are you?" I asked.

"I'm Ibrahim! Let's go! Let's go!"

"Our fee first."

"Yes, yes—after the conference," he muttered, trying to hurry us into the room.

"Absolutely not," I said resolutely.

"You can't do that!" He was flabbergasted.

"No? Watch me."

My years under Communism and my time in Israel had trained me to take a tough stand. I might have been naïve and trusting in the past, like a child mesmerized by the quick movements of a magician, ignoring telltale signs—but no longer. I would know from now on never to assume a negotiation was valid, even if a contract had been "signed."

Reluctantly, Ibrahim agreed, telling me to come with him. Hesitant to go alone, I asked my tour manager who happened to tower over the petite Ibrahim at 6 feet, 4 inches to accompany me. He hurried us to the administrative offices, opened the safe, and—*voila!*—placed the $50,000 in cash on the table. Then, Ibrahim offered us the ritual coffee that precedes any sale or exchange. Cautiously, we exchanged pleasantries and drank the coffee, tension filling the room and all eyes trained on the pile of large bills sitting at its center. At last, he officially handed me the money, my fee. As relief flooded, a hilarious postscript to the moment occurred when a bureaucrat came running after us to tug on my sleeve and request the fifty cents for coffee which was, evidently, not covered by Ibrahim's hospitality.

I have no doubt that had I not held up the press conference, the money would never have appeared. Our fee would have been swept away into the Egyptian sand dunes.

That wasn't the only hitch. Security was tight on opening night because Mrs. Mubarak and her friends were attending. When I arrived with the cast, we were confronted by six plainclothes policemen guarding the stage door. They refused to let us in because they "did not have instructions" to do so.

"Well, there won't be a show if you don't let us in," I warned them. "These are the performers!"

It took a lot of cajoling and pleading, but finally they opened the door—though they forced us all to leave our cell phones with them. Perhaps they feared the devices would trigger explosives.

Despite these appalling incidents, the government did hold a lovely reception on the terrace of the opera house before curtain on opening night. When it ended, Phyllis and I left the opera house, relieved that things seemed to be under control and going smoothly. We strolled to the other side of the plaza, enjoying the warm and tranquil evening.

Suddenly, we caught sight of a young American couple who appeared quite distraught. They were being refused entrance to the opera house because the man wasn't wearing a jacket.

"I'm so sorry to hear that," I told them. "Would you like to come back tomorrow evening?"

"But we already lost our tickets," the man protested.

"I'm the producer," I explained, "and I'd be delighted to give you two tickets for tomorrow's show."

The couple's disbelief turned to delight when they realized it was a real offer. What a wonderful end to a trying day. It was also a reminder that my presence on tour could make a real difference on many fronts—all of them unexpected. After all the maddening events of the day, seeing these eager theatergoers turned away from the opera house had been the final straw, and it was a true delight to surprise this young couple by restoring their tickets in a chance encounter. Their story brought all my own memories of life under an oppressive government regime, with its endless irrational bureaucratic rules, rushing back. I felt renewed gratitude to be an American now! I was tickled by this serendipitous moment that had offered a chance to take a small stand against tedious bureaucratic rules. Communism was full of closed doors, bureaucracy at every turn, and, here, at last, I could open at least one door for others.

The show was very well received, and the rest of the week was uneventful. The American Embassy hosted a delightful reception for the cast, where I was introduced to some of the Egyptian elite, a cordial, erudite group who welcomed me warmly. After that, Phyllis and I took off for a three-day tour down the Nile. I left Egypt relieved that my show had been a success but disappointed by the encounters I'd had there. There was one exception, however—Phyllis and I both adored the worldly Egyptologist who took us on a fabulous and informative tour of Cairo.

Riding in a taxi to the hotel, I noted that we were crossing "The October Bridge." I asked the driver, who spoke English, what the name meant. The title, he explained, commemorated Egypt's "great victory over the Jews in 1973." I was flabbergasted. I knew the truth of the October War. It was a feeble, failed attempt by Egypt to avenge their humiliating loss to Israel in 1967. (I was particularly sensitive to this piece of history in part because it had caused me to miss President Carter, who was at Camp David negotiating the peace agreement between Israel and Egypt in March of 1979, when I presented Maestro Segovia at the White House.) Evidently, naming the bridge was a way to save face after a war that cost thousands of lives on both sides.

Seeing the Pyramids and other grand historic sites such as Abu Simbel contrasted dramatically with the dispiriting interactions that permeated our Egyptian journey. Everyone, it seemed, had their hand out for a bribe. Museums demanded not just entrance fees but additional fees to enter specific exhibits. When we reached Aswan, we headed to a lovely hotel with a terrace for lunch, only to be stopped by a guard who wanted us to tip him just for the privilege of entering the place. I refused to pay, on principle. Phyllis thought I was overreacting. She tipped and entered with her friend Arlene while I stalked off and eventually entered the café through the garden, 300 feet away. After so many incidences of bad faith in my dealings with the opera house in Cairo, I could not submit to bribing a guard just to enter a hotel lobby! Childhood memories of similar outrages would always loom large enough to make me chafe at similar acts of bad faith.

I flew back to New York on the night before Passover. Onboard, the ironies continued. I was seated next to Ambassador Daniel Kurtzer, our generous host in Cairo, who had been the driving force behind our tour. We started chatting. He reassured me that despite the challenges of being paid and the organizational snafus, our tour had been a big success. It starkly contrasted with his own attempt to bring *Sesame Street* to the children of Egypt, he explained. After raising some $10 million to translate the popular TV show into Arabic, with the owners generously waiving royalties, the tapes arrived at the Embassy. The consulate contacted the Department of Cultural Affairs to arrange a ceremony for the handover and to acknowledge the goodwill and generosity of the U.S., only to be told that the department needed an additional $1 million. The ambassador was shocked. They wanted *money in addition to* the generous gift they had already received? "Well," explained the Egyptians, "if you Americans could raise $10 million for this project, what is $1 million more to you?!" The tapes, the Ambassador told me, were now languishing on a shelf in the American Embassy.

Building Bridges

The Peoples' Great Hall, Beijing, December 2001

After the Egyptian experience, I was primed for the unexpected. I had been to China before working with Hsu Po-yun, a Taiwan presenter. Colleagues had warned me that the Chinese "don't like to pay" the last portion of their contracts. I couldn't imagine they would not respect the contract, but, in fact, this was exactly what happened. When I made plans for a tour of *Porgy and Bess* in 2001, I thought I knew what to expect: I assumed I wouldn't get the last portion of the payment, so I built it into the first tranche.

The *Porgy* company of sixty-five and I were in Singapore for two performances at the Esplanade Opera House a few days before we were due to arrive in Beijing. I received an unexpected call from my Chinese contacts announcing that we would be able to do only one performance in the People's Great Hall rather than the two we were contracted for, because the Communist party was meeting during the second date.

"We have a contract!" I said. "We are already at your doorstep. It's impossible to change at this late date!"

"I'm so sorry, but we have no choice," my contact told me. "The party gives the directive. Mr. Klein, we are very much looking forward to your arrival."

I had no way to reverse their decision. Once again, I had to concede defeat to the Communist party! I tried to mollify myself: they weren't, after all, *canceling* the engagement altogether, and the American Embassy was still planning a reception for the evening before the performance. I was still bringing an American masterpiece to the Chinese, and the most hallowed venue in China. Still, I dreaded breaking the news to my cast.

The Chinese built according to our instructions a replica of our scenery, except, in size, it was made much larger to fill the proportions of the enormous stage. The theater, The People's Great Hall, has some 10,000 seats. The scenery may have been proportional to the venue's stage now, but the size of the set created a real challenge for the cast.

I was immensely grateful to them for handling the adjustment professionally and with a sense of optimism, despite how little time they had to adjust. We were finally granted access to the theater only on the afternoon of the performance. We arrived two hours before the show to prepare. I knew the scale in numbers, but to actually experience it was something else. The actors, however, were thrilled by the space, if overwhelmed by it, and excited to perform in such a revered setting, the seat of power in China!

At the embassy reception the evening before, an assistant to Li Lanqing, the minister of culture and vice-premier of China, had approached and invited me and "the representatives of the company" (a phrase often used by Communists) to a personal meeting before the performance. I selected the conductor and the two lead actors to accompany me. Half an hour before show time, we were escorted to a grand reception hall with enormous wingback armchairs.

"We would like to welcome you and your company," an interpreter translated. He pointed to a chair in the center of a U-shaped arrangement of armchairs and indicated that I should sit with Li Lanqing. Once seated, I noticed that a famous painting of Mao leading the people was hanging on the wall in front of me. In the first few minutes of our conversation, the minister used the two interpreters, but before long, he relaxed and started speaking fluent English. Eventually, he dismissed both interpreters. Vice-premier Li grew animated and told me of his dream of visiting New York. He asked many questions about George Gershwin. I was very surprised by the degree of his curiosity about the composer and equally delighted by his depth of knowledge. He was fascinated by every detail of my friendship with Frances Gershwin, George's sister, who had died two years earlier. Our animated conversation continued past curtain time, despite my politely pointing out that it was past show time.

"Don't worry," he assured me. "They'll wait for me."

Our riveting conversation continued for another fifteen minutes, though I was so worried about the delay that I scarcely remember

Building Bridges

what was discussed in that time. At last Li noted my anxiety. "Let us proceed," he said.

We were escorted down several long hallways, several secret-service men hovering. Li Lanqing and I entered the Great Hall auditorium through a side door. The moment we walked in, all 10,000 people jumped to their feet as though one. An usher escorted us to our seats, which were the equivalent of a royal box. Ironically, the Communist "aristocracy" held court in an even more theatrical manner than did those in the West.

The performance received a standing ovation and much more enthusiasm than I expected, but there was no backstage contact after the show. When I finally returned to my hotel room and called Phyllis to tell her about the experience, I realized it had all seemed unreal. It stills seems incredible that I was hosted by the second-in-command of the billion and a half Chinese people, having escaped from Communism myself thirty-two years earlier.

There were other tours of note. In 2008, the audiences in both St. Petersburg and Moscow greeted the show enthusiastically, but the difficult people behind-the-scenes made our experience in Russia a dreadful one. Sometime later, I found out from my friend and colleague Patricia Murray-Bett that Vladimir Kekhman, the presenter in St. Petersburg, had served time in jail for importing not only performances but . . . also heroin. Not surprisingly, he paid me only part of what our contract stipulated. That wasn't the only mishap in Russia. One of my Porgys missed the second performance because his driver drove him to the wrong location, and we couldn't find him! Our actor was convinced the driver had been instructed to do this deliberately, though what the motive might have been remains a mystery. Still, I'm glad I had the opportunity to visit Russia—particularly the Hermitage, where my daughter Alexis arranged a private tour through her contacts at Sotheby's. I was even more relieved to get my cast safely *out* of Russia. Some ten years later, I felt vindicated when some twenty Western countries expelled their Russian diplomats in response to the poisoning on U.K. soil of ex-spy Sergei Skripal and his daughter, Yulia.

These experiences were etched in my memory because they highlighted not only the challenges of performing in a foreign land but the kaleidoscopic confusion that can occur when cultures collide—and sometimes connect. I organized 1,225 performances of *Porgy and Bess* around the globe, more than 90 percent of which took place in Western countries. In the West, we were paid without incident. We had problems only with the handful of performances we did in Russia, Egypt, Estonia, China, Taiwan, and Greece.

My career has taught me that international diplomacy is complex and that art is often appreciated in unintended ways. *Porgy and Bess*, a "Black-life opera" presented as an American classic, is a good example. Audiences from other countries are bound to interpret the story through a different lens than do Americans, since most have no firsthand experience of America's long-standing, deeply contentious, and often confusing struggle with Black/White relations and institutional racism. Despite the frequently frayed fabric of this undertaking, I believe in the power of the performing arts as a bridge between cultures. It's ironic that the State Department invested so much in the arts during the Cold War—and *now* it's a struggle to keep any funding alive. To underestimate the effect of something as seemingly ephemeral as music and dance on the citizenry of a country is to overlook one of the government's most important—and opulent—resources.

18
Harmony in Israel

I brought *Porgy and Bess* to Israel twice, and both were moving experiences. The first took place at Caesarea, a majestic Roman amphitheater north of Tel Aviv near the Mediterranean, in 1994, not far from where my family lived when we first arrived in Israel. Shortly before this event, I was informed that Ezer Weizman, Israel's president, would be in the audience. Weizman had been commander of the Israeli air force during the 1967 Six Day War, which I remembered only too well. To my delight, Mr. Weizman came backstage at intermission. When he greeted me in English, I responded in Hebrew, and called him "Ha-Mefaked," which means "Commander," to honor his military achievements and great contributions to Israel. He was delighted, and then dismayed to learn I'd "abandoned" the Jewish homeland. Only later did I learn that our exchange had been filmed for Israeli TV! I still have a photo from that interchange.

In 2001, I again presented *Porgy*, this time at the Mishkan Opera House, Israel's prime performing-arts venue. This was in the midst of the second *intifada*, and my cast was awfully nervous about traveling here. A number of foreign groups, including an English soccer team, had just canceled visits to Israel, which added to the excitement of the press when we decided to come, regardless of the heightened threat. As ticket sales were brisk, the run was extended from fourteen to seventeen performances. At the final performance, I wanted to surprise the audience with something special, so the cast and orchestra rehearsed the popular song "Hevenu Shalom Alechem," which means "we brought peace upon you." I taught them all the words, and after the final performance, as they were taking their bows, they performed it. The audience erupted in cheers and sang along with my cast. It was one of those moments in a long career of thrills and novel experiences that transcended regular life. A sense of unity and peace fell over the theater. I thought of the moment I first set foot in Israel—eighteen years old, bewildered, and lost. How recent it seemed, and also how long ago. At rare moments like this, all the stresses and challenges of my life and work seemed to fade away.

Two decades into touring *Porgy and Bess*, the cultural climate had begun to shift. When I started touring the production, I was able to produce it for well under a million dollars and still have a reasonable return. But after the global financial crisis of 2008–2009, state support for the arts drastically dwindled. Other funding sources dried up as well. There was a cultural sea change, too—declining interest in opera and other classical forms made my line of work less fruitful. At the same time, costs increased, making touring riskier and more difficult. Not only that, but the Internet was making the impresario all but obsolete. No longer did one need Elias Grappa to find a connection in the United States; no longer was it about the gift of negotiation and talent scouting, stirring up competition among venues, nursing relationships with management and theater companies. It was curtains for touring *Porgy*—and, in many ways, for me as an impresario, although I did continue to do some tours, including *Ain't Misbehavin'* in seven European countries. Still, the new century was redefining performing-arts management.

Decades of touring George Gershwin's masterpiece brought joy to many people around the world. I felt especially gratified by the shift in

Harmony in Israel

our audiences over the years. When we first began touring, we rarely saw anyone of color in attendance. Black people had initially been critical of a show that depicted them as struggling and destitute. With so little representation, this depiction was even more potentially troubling. As years went by, we saw many more Black people in the audience, enthusiastic and accepting, not to mention appropriating much of Gershwin's music into the jazz idiom. I considered this approval no less than an act of grace, an honor bestowed on our company, and on Gershwin himself. This was no small gift, and as my career as an impresario was winding down, these sorts of happy memories became my greatest bounty.

19
Reflections

My journey continues at a reflective pace in this fast-paced world. I thought of writing this memoir because I wanted to capture many of the stories with which I'd entertained friends and family over the decades. In the process, I became more aware of the significance of the timing of my exporting American performing arts to Europe and the rest of the world. The American creative energy and the confidence of our musical genres of contemporary dance, Broadway musicals, Gospel and jazz were embraced with anticipation and excitement worldwide.

I have recently worked as a consultant to several American-style musicals created and launched in Italy. Sadly, none of the three have gone much further than a brief run in London, orchestrated by impresario Patricia Murray Bett. *Napoletango* received good reviews but was not a box office success. The cost of launching a musical without a known star or a name playwright can be prohibitive, not to mention the many other challenges. Another musical, *Celeste*, is a contemporary story of Lucifer landing in Rome, where a woman named Celeste saves him from being hit by a bus. Despite its positive response in Rome, it never received backing for an extended run or tour, even with an English stage director. There are many factors such as star draw and musical themes, but cultural differences are perhaps still the most critical.

Recently, my eight-year old grandson, Léo and I were playing chess. He is getting better with every game. It's our ritual; he has patience for it in a way I might not have had when I was small. So many things are different, though, about his life in New York City in 2022 than they were for me in mid-century Timișoara. My childhood was marked by a driving impatience to see the world; he and his sister, Elodie, wake up with the world at their feet. Maybe this isn't an entirely good thing, but for me as a grandfather, it makes me very happy.

I first set foot in New York on a steamy August day in 1968 and instantly felt the city's quicksilver energy coursing through me. All the reports were true—in the air hung a sense of infinite possibility. In fact, New York City seems to be built on the very concept of the future. It was certainly the frontier for the performing arts when I arrived and made a career of exporting them. New York City is still as much an immigrant hub as it was when I arrived here in 1968, still an explosion of dialects and cultures and emotional intensity. It is still exciting and fast-paced. New Yorkers talk fast and walk fast; they even make friends fast—in bodegas, on street corners, playing with their kids in the park. This is my daughters' childhood, their homeland, their culture; here is where two of my grandchildren collect their landmarks and their memories, their understanding of how time works, how life is paced, which direction we look—which is forward. "Go forth unafraid," the Dalton School urges.

Writing this memoir was, of course, a process of looking back. This meant re-living nightmarish episodes and coming to terms with the pathos and tragedies of a time and country that feel a universe away from my living room overlooking the Hudson River. I wanted to understand things, to see the connections one draws only in re-telling, to see the story connecting the discrete episodes that make up a life. I wanted to tell the tale of how one immigrant came to America and, with some help and

Reflections

some luck and some hard work, became not only American himself, but a spokesman for this country. How does such a thing happen? How do you begin life as a Hungarian Jew in Romania, on the outside, reduced, stripped, fearing a bleak future—and end up marrying a sophisticated, modern New Yorker, traveling the world representing world-famous dance companies and musical-theater masterpieces? How was I so lucky? Many others with as much talent and skill have gambled on the land of opportunity and lost. Timing was everything. Privilege helped a great deal. Speaking a lot of languages played an essential role. Feeling I had nothing to lose—this was a big part of it, too.

At the time of this writing, the world has been seized by a pandemic of terrifying proportions. Even in New York City, the future feels less a guarantee; plans feel theoretical at best. I have experienced the dizzying sensation of culture shock before, fleeing the Iron Curtain and arriving in Israel, then Europe, then New York, each so different from the other. I have lived long enough to feel eras shift slowly, like tectonic plates. Now I have seen an era shift almost overnight—as have we all who have watched the city shut down, fighting valiantly against this plague. In this strange lockdown world, we can feel that our actions are either idle or more urgent than ever.

Writing this memoir, I was forced to reflect upon the tapestry of my life and the threads that fueled my actions and challenges. Unquestionably my multi-ethnic background and linguistic expertise enhanced my understanding of cultural divides and possible bridges that could be built.

Scientists are now sharing globally at an unprecedented rate in the fight against Covid-19. This was the great lesson of my career: It is only when nations share their best that the world moves forward. It is not just our institutions, either scientific or artistic, that secure our future, but the bridges we must tirelessly build among them.

Of course, I want my grandchildren to look to the future, but I also want to say, *look to the past*. Look at these things that happened before you and made you possible. Look back at the Old World so you better understand the new. Here you hold the prequel to your life—now, go make a lot of that life, take chances, honor the great-great-grandmother kidnapped by the Romanian secret police, and the great-grandfather who, after surviving a labor camp, made educating his sons his life's work. From him, Gabriel and I learned geography and music and literature and language, and because of it, we had not only knowledge, but ambition and dreams. This made all the difference. Your decisions may make all the difference, too. Look backward before you gallop into the future.

We had a little garden behind our house in Timișoara, before the house was taken from us. The grandchildren in that garden might have been my grandchildren, in another universe. Instead, in August, 2001 we contracted to buy a Villa in Fiesole outside of Florence and despite the skepticism of friends and family, after 9/11 proceeded to purchase our Villa il Sogno, in March, 2002. We restored the home with its surrounding gardens with orchards and olive trees too! We have loved planting seeds there in every way—watching the fruit and vegetable patches grow over time couldn't be a more apt metaphor for beginning again, as I have done many times in the past. Our Italian home is a tranquil, rural paradise, but it comes with all the vagaries one would expect—some draining, some infuriating, some funny. *Viva Italia!* When we are not in New York, we are there, and our grandchildren play in these gardens with us.

50 Years of Tours and Productions

YEAR	PRODUCTION	COUNTRY
1973–1974	"Dreyfus on Devil's Island" by Michael Almaz—Hunter College/Kaye Playhouse and Tour.	USA
1974	"Madame Butterfly", Metropolitan Opera Touring Company; "To Live Another Summer" a Musical, Rod Rodgers (1938–2002) Dance Company; Masters Festival of the Performing Arts (6 weeks), Masters School, Dobby Ferry, NY.	USA
1974	"A Rose is a Rose, is a Rose" and "Sarah Bernhardt" 2 One Woman Shows by Stephanie Rich—Tour.	USA
1974	I Solisti di Zagreb (Chamber Group)—Tour.	USA
1975	Michael Lorimer, Master Guitarist, Tour.	Israel
1976	"Ambakaila", the Trinidad Folklore Group, Aubrey Adams (1919–2007)—Spoleto and Tour.	Italy
1977	American Ballet Theater with Mikhail Baryshnikov—The Nervi Festival, Genova 07/07/1977.	Italy
1977	Guillermo Fierens, Guitarist—Harvard Club, Boston.	USA
1977	Israel Ballet, Tour.	USA, Canada
1977	Ballet Folklorica de Mexico—Tour.	Italy
1977–1978	"Porgy and Bess"—the HGO Production—Tour.	Italy, France
1978	"The Dybbuk", Pearl Lang (1921–2009)—The Nervi Festival and Tour.	Italy
1978	Asami Maki Ballet of Tokyo—Tour.	Italy, Israel, France, UK
1978	Leslie Brown and Friends (star of the movie "Turning Point")—Tour.	Israel, South Africa
1979	Andres Segovia (1893–1987) The White House—March 11, 1979.	USA

YEAR	PRODUCTION	COUNTRY
1979	The Boston Ballet—Artistic Director: E. Virginia Williams (1914–1984)—The Nervi Festival and Tour.	Italy
1979	Erick Hawkins (1909–1994) Dance Company—The Nervi Festival and Tour.	Italy
1979	"Crowsnest", Martha Clark, Felix Blaska, Robert Barnett—Spoleto and Tour.	Italy
1979	Arnie Zane (1948–1988) & Bill T. Jones Company—Tour.	Italy
1979	Les Ballets Trockadero de Monte Carlo of New York—Spoleto and Tour.	Italy, Israel
1980	The National Ballet of Canada—Artistic Director: Erik Bruhn (1928-1986)—The Nervi Festival.	Italy
1980	The Feld Ballet, Artistic Director: Eliot Feld—The Nervi Festival and Tour.	Italy, France
1980	Asami Maki Ballet of Tokyo, Soloist: Arènes de Cimiez—Nice and Tour.	France
1980	Dance Theater of Harlem—Artistic Director: Arthur Mitchell—London	England
1981	"West Side Story"—the 1980 Nederlander Broadway production; David Stahl (1949–2010) Conductor—The Nervi Festival and Tour.	Italy, France, Monte Carlo
1981	The Boston Ballet—Artistic Director: E. Virginia Williams (1914–1984)—Tour.	Israel
1981	Dance Theater of Harlem—Spoleto, Tel Aviv.	Italy, Israel
1981	Alexander Godunov (1949–1995) with Israel Ballet—Herodus Aticus, Athens.	Greece
1981	"Hair" the Musical, a Till Polla (1946-2012) Production—Tour.	Italy, Israel
1981	"Il Trovatore", "Madama Butterfly" (Company of 210), The Genova Opera—Caesarea and Jerusalem.	Israel

50 Years of Tours and Productions

YEAR	PRODUCTION	COUNTRY
1981	Oakland Dance Company—The Nervi Festival and Tour.	Italy
1982	Gail Conrad Tap Dance—Torino and Tour.	Italy
1982–1987	The Feld Ballet, Artistic Director: Eliot Feld. Several Tours.	Italy
1982	Bob Bowyer (1947–1992) and Joann Bruggeman (1931–2013)—Tour.	Italy
1982	"Grease" the Musical—a Till Polla (1946-2012) Production—Tour.	Italy
1982	Alexander Godunov (1949–1995) and Friends—Teatro Teresa Carreño, Caracas.	Venezuela
1982	The José Limón (1908–1972) Dance Company—Reggio Emilia and Tour.	Italy
1982	Marie Brooks (1929–2013) Children's Theatre—Tour.	Italy
1982	Alvin Ailey (1931–1989) American Dance Theater—Tour.	Italy, Israel
1982–2002	"West Side Story" Bernstein (1918-1990); Robbins (1918-1998); Laurents (1917-2011)—Several Tours.	Israel, France, Italy
1982	"Ain't Misbehavin'" New Musical direct from New York—Milano, Firenze and Tour.	Italy
1983	Marie Brooks (1929–2013) Children's Theatre—Return Engagement Tour.	Italy
1983	Twyla Tharp Dance Company—Caesarea.	Israel
1983	Alvin Ailey (1931–1989) American Dance Theater—Return Engagement Tour.	Israel
1983	Alexander Godunov (1949–1995) and Eva Evdokimova (1948-2009)—Cannes, Nice.	France
1983	The San Francisco Ballet—Spoleto and Tour, Caesarea, Athens.	Italy, Israel, Greece
1983	Alexander Godunov (1949–1995) and Eva Evdokimova (1948-2009)—with Israel Ballet—Tour.	Israel

YEAR	PRODUCTION	COUNTRY
1983	*The Feld Ballet—Spoleto and Tour.*	Italy
1984	Ohad Naharin, Dancer/Choreographer— *E Lucean le Stelle Festival, Roma.*	Italy
1984	*Byakko Sha of Kyoto—Spoleto and Tour.*	Italy, Germany
1984	Alvin Ailey (1931-1989) American Dance Theater—Tour.	Italy
1984	"New York Express"—a PK Production (Introducing Breakdance to Europe)—Spoleto Festival and Tour.	Italy
1984	*Ballet Hispanico of New York—Torino Fiera FIAT.*	Italy
1984	*Israel Ballet—Santiago de Chile and Tour.*	USA, Canada, Chile
1984	"Hair" the Musical, Teatro Ciak—Milano and Tour.	Italy
1984	"Hair" the Musical—a PK Production, European Tour.	Italy, France, Switzerland, Spain, Austria, Germany
1985	"Bubbling Brown Sugar"—Tour.	Italy, Belgium
1985	*Mummenschanz—Tour.*	South Africa
1985	*The National Ballet of Canada—Presented by La Scala, Milano.*	Italy
1985	"Jesus Christ Superstar" the Musical; a Till Polla (1946-2011) Production.	Italy
1985	"Rush Dance"; Patrice M. Regnier, Choreographer—Tour.	Italy
1985	*Lee Theodore's (1933–1987) American Dance Machine—Spoleto, Teatro Sistina—Roma and Tour.*	Italy
1985	"Rigoletto", "Il Barbiere di Siviglia"—Starring Giorgio Lormi—Tour.	Israel
1985	"Jesus Christ Superstar" the Musical; with Pierre Arty (1923-2010), Brussels.	Belgium

50 Years of Tours and Productions

YEAR	PRODUCTION	COUNTRY
1985	"Gershwin!" by Festival Dance Theater—Reggio Emilia and Tour.	Italy
1986	"Parker & Pucci" ex Pilobolus—Tour.	Italy
1986	"A Chorus Line"—Michael Bennett (1943–1987) European Premiere—The Nervi Festival, Puccini Festival and Tour.	Italy
1986	"Swan Lake"—La Scala Ballet, by Franco Zeffirelli (Company of 180)—Lorin Maazel (1930–2014)—Tour.	USA, Canada
1986	The Sydney Ballet of Australia—Spoleto.	Italy
1987	"ITALY IN HOUSTON" Celebrating opening of the Italian Consulate in Houston.	USA
1987	Bella Lewitzky (1916–2004) Dance Company—Tour.	Italy
1987	Gerry Mulligan (1927–1996), Jazz Saxophone—La Fenice Opera House, Venice.	Italy
1987	Les Ballets Russes de Monte Carlo, by Princess Grace (1929–1982)—Tour.	USA, Canada
1987	"The Fantasticks"—a PK Production, La Fenice Opera House, Venice.	Italy
1988	The Joffrey Ballet, Artistic Director: Gerald Arpino (1928-2008) with Dr. Konrad Schilling (1927–2016)—Duisburg.	Germany
1988	Keith Jarrett, Jazz Pianist—Budapest.	Hungary
1988	Pilobolus Dance Theater—Tour.	Israel
1988	"Esther, A Vaudeville Megillah" Musical by Elizabeth Swados (1951–2016)—Teatro Pier Lombardo, Milano and Tour.	Italy
1988	Ohad Naharin, Dancer/Choreographer—Spoleto.	Italy
1988	"Boston Pops at La Fenice", Michel Sasson (1936–2013) conductor—La Fenice Opera House, Venice.	Italy

THE LAST IMPRESARIO

YEAR	PRODUCTION	COUNTRY
1988	"The Works" by Jennifer Muller, with Dr. Konrad Schilling (1927–2016)—Duisburg.	Germany
1988	American Choreographers at Maggio Musicale, Firenze Opera House.	Italy
1988-1997	"Il Barbiere di Siviglia"; "Cavalleria Rusticana"/"I Pagliacci"; "Tosca"; "Rigoletto"—Opera Nazionale Italiana, a PK and Francesco Stochino Weiss Production: .	USA, Canada
1988–1993	ATER Balletto of Italy—Tour.	USA
1989	Martha Graham (1894–1991) Dance Company—Tour.	Hong Kong
1989	The National Ballet of Spain, Artistic Director: Maya Plisetskaya (1925–2015)—National Arts Center, Taipei.	Taiwan
1989	Mummenschanz, Founder: Andres Bossard (1944—1992)—Tour.	Israel
1989	"Mama, I Want to Sing!"—the Longest Running Off Broadway Black Musical. By Vy Higgensen & Ken Wydro—Tour.	Italy, Greece, Slovenia, Turkey, Austria
1989	"Let the Music Play Gospel" by Vy Higgensen & Ken Wydro—Tour.	Italy, Turkey, Greece, Slovenia, Austria
1989	Ballet Hispanico of New York—Artistic Director: Tina Ramirez.	Italy
1989	"Buona Fortuna" a PK Production, Director George Faison, with Gene Anthony Ray (1962–2003) and Company (FAME TV series)—Tour.	Italy
1990	"TAMARA"—the Play You Follow from Room to Room. Villa Brasini, Roma; Villa Erba, Como.	Italy
1990	Gregg Smith Singers—Cagliari, Sardegna.	Italy
1990	Ballet Folklorico de Mexico—Amalia Hernandez (1917–2000)—Tour.	Spain

50 Years of Tours and Productions

YEAR	PRODUCTION	COUNTRY
1990	"Blues in the Night" the Musical, Sheldon Epps. Buenos Aires.	Argentina
1990	"Esther, A Vaudeville Megillah" a Musical by Elizabeth Swados (1951-2016)—Tour.	Spain, Italy
1991	"Cosi Fan' Tutte" with Francesco Stochino Weiss. Madrid.	Spain
1991	"Oh! Calcutta", a Till Polla (1946–2012) Production—Tour.	Italy
1991	"Rigoletto", "Il Barbiere di Siviglia"—Opera Nazionale Italiana—a PK & Francesco Stochino Weiss Production. Michel Sasson (1936–2013), Conductor—Mexico City, Guadalahara, Lisbon.	Mexico, Portugal
1991	*Ballet Folklorico de Mexico—Amalia Hernandez (1917–2000)—Tour.*	Israel
1992	"Porgy and Bess" Teatro Colon, Buenos Aires; Teatro Municipal Sao Paolo; Teatro Solís, Montevideo.	Angentina, Brazil, Uruguay
1992	"Broadway Tonite" by Mara Joyce—Tour.	Japan
1992	"The Works", by Jennifer Muller—The Nervi Festival.	Italy
1992	*The Joffrey Ballet; Artistic Director: Gerald Arpino (1923–2008),—Palermo.*	Italy
1992	*Robert Desrosiers Dance Company of Toronto—Spoleto.*	Italy
1992	*The Pittsburgh Ballet—National Arts Center, Taipei.*	Taiwan

YEAR	PRODUCTION	COUNTRY
1992-2013	"PORGY AND BESS"—a PK Touring Production: 1,224 shows, 25 countries, 6 continents.	USA, Argentina, Brazil, Canada Mexico, Trinidad, Uruguay, Estonia, Greece, Hungary, Ireland, Latvia, Poland, Portugal, Russia, UK, China, Hong Kong, Israel, Japan, Singapore, Taiwan, Australia, New Zealand, Egypt.
1993	"The Works" by Jennifer Muller—Tour.	Germany, Andorra
1993	National Philippine Folklore Ballet -Tour.	USA
1994	Philadelphia Children's Theater—National Arts Center, Taipei.	Taiwan
1994	"Broadway Tonite" by Mara Joyce, Zurich.	Switzerland
1994	Victoria Chaplin & Jean Baptiste Thierrée—Festival Cervantino.	Mexico
1995	"Harlem Gospel"—Belem Opera House, Lisbon.	Portugal
1996	The Joffrey Ballet; Artistic Director: Gerald Arpino (1923–2008)—Torino.	Italy
1996	Grupo Corpo of Bello Horizonte—7th Biennale de la Danse, Lyon.	France
1997	"Broadway Tonite" by Mara Joyce—Taormina, Sicily.	Italy
1997	"Porgy and Bess" Singers—Bregenz.	Austria
1997-2001	Makiko Hirata, Pianist—Budapest, U.S. Tour.	Hungary, USA

50 Years of Tours and Productions

YEAR	PRODUCTION	COUNTRY
1998	"Broadway Tonite" by Mara Joyce—Tour.	Switzerland, Japan, Hong Kong
1998	"Rigoletto", Opera Nazionale Italiana, a PK & Francesco Stochino Weiss Production—Tour.	Portugal
1998	Makiko Hirata, Pianist—Weill Recital Hall, New York.	USA
1999	David Helfgott—Belem Opera House, Lisbon.	Portugal
1999	Makiko Hirata, Pianist with Pécs Orchestra, Pécs.	Hungary
2000	Whitney Houston (1963–2012) Tel Aviv wedding. (Contract canceled last minute).	Israel
2001–2005	Pécs Symphony Orchestra, Hungary—Péter Szkládanyi (1948- 2003) Conductor.	USA
2001	"Viva Verdi 2001"—a PK Production, with Patricia Murray-Bett—Tour.	UK, Ireland
2002	The ARAD Symphony Orchestra, Dorin Frandes, Conductor—Tour.	USA, Canada
2003	Resovia Symphony Orchestra of Poland—Tour.	USA
2003	The Shanghai Acrobats of China—Tour.	USA, Bermuda
2004	"Broadway Tonite" by Mara Joyce—Warsaw.	Poland
2004	"Titanic the Musical", a John Hodge Production—Tour.	Japan
2005	National Philippine Folklore Ballet—Tour.	USA
2005	"A Couple of Blaguards" Frank (1930–2009) and Malachy McCourt—Tour.	Australia, New Zealand
2005	Merce Cunningham (1919-2009) Dance Company—Cagliari, Sardegna.	Italy
2007	Leopold Gershwin Godowsky (1938–2011), Pianist—Resovia.	Poland
2007	Liza Minnelli—Taormina Amphitheater, Sicily.	Italy
2007	The Kibbutz Dance Company of Israel—The Joyce Theater, New York & Tour.	USA, Canada

THE LAST IMPRESARIO

YEAR	PRODUCTION	COUNTRY
2008	"Nam Van Lake", Studio Festi—Macau, May 1–3; Pre-Beijing Olympic Games Spectacular.	Macau
2008–2009	*Janice Martin, Pianist, Violinist, Singer, Aerialist—Tour.*	USA
2009–2015	"The Gate of Harmony", Studio Festi.	Macau
2010	*Ruth Palmer, Violinist. Stradivarius Program—Villa La Pietra, Firenze.*	Italy
2010	"Carmen", Antonio Gades (1936–2004) Dance Company—Tour.	Israel
2010	"Napoletango" of Italy—The Coliseum Theater, London, with Patricia Murray-Bett.	England
2010	Flash Mob with Antonio Vanni, Opera al Mercato, S. Ambrogio, Firenze.	Italy
2011	"Bodas de Sangre", Antonio Gades (1936–2004) Dance Company—Tour.	Israel
2011	*The Israel Ballet—Tour*	USA, Canada
2011–2012	"Ain't Misbehavin'"—a PK Production—Tour.	France, Germany, Greece, Hungary, Israel, Italy, Spain, Turkey
2012	"Broadway in Florence"—Villa La Pietra, Firenze	Italy
2012	Studio Festi Project 2012, Dubai.	United Arab Emirates
2013	*Los Vivancos, of Spain in Budapest, London.*	Hungary, England
2013–2018	*Armel Budapest Orchestras with Patricia Murray-Bett—Tour.*	UK, Ireland, France
2015	*Peking Opera of Beijing—Lincoln Center, New York; Kennedy Center Opera House, Washington, D.C.*	USA

50 Years of Tours and Productions

YEAR	PRODUCTION	COUNTRY
2014	The Maszka Band of Budapest, with Los Vivancos—Tour.	Spain, Italy
2014	Los Vivancos—National Bejing TV for Chinese New Year, (1 billion viewers)—Beijing.	China
2014	"Porgy and Bess"—PAB Production—Palacio Bellas Artes, Mexico City.	Mexico
2014–2018	Armel Bands, Budapest, touring with World on Stage Productions, 200+ shows—Tour.	UK, Ireland
2015	Los Vivancos, with Patricia Murray-Bett, Jersey Opera House.	UK
2015-2018	"Celeste" Italian Musical, in production—Roma.	Italy
2017	The Budapest Virtuosi 2017—Weill Recital Hall, Carnegie Hall, New York.	USA
2018	The Budapest Virtuosi 2018—Weill Recital Hall, Carnegie Hall, New York.	USA
2018	Armel Octet with Bill T. Jones Company—Florence Dance Festival	Italy
2019	New York Brass a PK Production—Weill Recital Hall, Carnegie Hall, New York	USA
2020	Covid	
2021	Florence Dance Festival—Commissione Artistica	Italy
2022	Callas' Caleidoscope—Senior Advisor	Italy
2022	Florence Dance Festival—Commissione Artistica	Italy

Notes

Prologue

1. Baryshnikov, Mikhail. https://www.britannica.com/biography/Mikhail-Baryshnikov.
2. Harris, Andrea. Nabokov, a close friend of Balanchine since the Ballet Russes, was one of the intellectuals who argued early that the U.S. needed to take much stronger cultural action to counteract Soviet propaganda in Europe. Clearly, exporting our artistic credibility was one way to enhance our cultural standing. *Making Ballet American: Modernism Before and Beyond Balenchine*, Oxford University Press, (2018), 167–170.

Chapter 1: Transylvania Revisited

1. *The Yivo Encyclopedia of Jews in Eastern Europe*: www.yivoencyclopedia.org/article.aspx/Timişoara.
2. Romania Tourism, 36 http://romaniatourism.com/Timişoara.html.
3. United States Holocaust Museum website: https://www.ushmm.org/research/scholarly-presentations/conferences/the-holocaust-in-hungary-70-years-later/the-holocaust-in-hungary-frequently-asked-questions.

4. *Holocaust Encyclopedia*, United States Holocaust Memorial Museum: https://www.ushmm.org/wlc/en/article.php?ModuleId =10005472.
5. https://en.wikipedia.org/wiki/1941_Odessa_massacre.
6. The World Holocaust Remembrance Center: http://www.yadvashem .org/holocaust/about/final-solution-beginning/romania.

Chapter 6: A Life-Altering Encounter

1. Hurok, Sol. Wikipedia: https://en.wikipedia.org › wiki › Sol_Hurok.
2. De Mille, Agnes. Wikipedia.
3. Segovia, Andrés. Wikipedia.
4. Bomb—Hurok office Fire Bomb Kills Woman, Hurts 13 in Hurok Office (Published 1972) *New York Times*. This was an indication of right-wing violence that was always simmering underneath an idealized democracy. https://www.nytimes.com › 1972/01/27 › archives › fire-b.
5. Nureyev, Rudolf. Wikepedia.

Chapter 7: The Birth of Living Arts

1. Hurok death on first page of *New York Times*, March 6, 1974 https: //timesmachine.nytimes.com/timesmachine/1974/03/06/79866236 .html?pageNumber=1.
2. The Communist Party was excluded entirely from government, with the partial exception of the short-lived Historic Compromise, in which the PCI (Partito Comunista Italiano) provided external support to a DC minority government from 1976 to 1979. In the face of the twin crises of the economy and terrorism, as well as the example of then recent military coup d'état in Chile that had toppled a Marxist government, the Communist Party, led by Enrico Berlinguer, adopted a policy in 1973 that he called the "historic compromise." It entailed more or less formal alliances between the Christian Democrats and the Communists for the good of the country. https://www.britannica .com/place/Italy/Politics-in-the-1970s-and-80s.

Notes

3. Ambakaila, a folk group from Trinidad created by Aubrey Adams, first toured with Hurok. After a successful run, this was the first group I chose to export in 1976. http://www.bestoftrinidad.com/profiles/adamsA.html.
4. For the first time in the history of the Biennale, American participation was under the sponsorship of the United States Information Agency, which commissioned the Jewish Museum in New York to prepare the exhibition. The exhibition they prepared was headed by Alan R. Solomon. Besides Rauschenberg, the American entrants were painters Morris Louis, Kenneth Noland, Jasper Johns, Jim Dine, and Frank Stella, and sculptors John Chamberlain and Claes Oldenburg. Solomon told *The New York Times*, "This is an exciting moment in our cultural history: no doubt it will generate a certain amount of controversy in Venice this summer." https://www.nytimes.com/1964/06/20/venice-prize-goes-to-rauschenberg.html.
5. Rauschenberg, Robert. This article highlights how Rauschenberg's controversial win of the Golden Lion upended the art world and put American contemporary art on the world stage with New York as the center. https://observer.com/2017/07/robert-rauschenberg-venice-biennale-documentary/.
6. Vaughan, David. Cunningham: 50 Years, Aperture, 2005. Vaughan highlights his surprise at the negative reaction in Paris in 1964 when the audience threw eggs and tomatoes on the stage of the Theatre de l'est after Rauschenberg won the Golden Lion. I would argue that it was precisely because Rauschenberg as the first American won the coveted award that the Parisians felt their artistic aesthetic was being threatened. (Interview at the Lincoln Center Library of Performing Arts, 2016.) Vaughan stated at the time he was surprised that highly cultivated people from the world of art and theater would react this way.
7. Jordan, Stephanie. "Invasion or Inspiration?" in American Dance Abroad. worldcat.org, 267. "In some art disciplines, there seems

to have been a resentment of nothing short of American cultural imperialism" which expands upon both Britain and the continent's reluctance to embrace American culture even in the late '60s.

Chapter 9: A Segovia Reprise

1. *Rodeo*, Harris, Andrea. Making Ballet American: Modernism Before and Beyond Balanchine, Oxford University Press, 2018, 148 and 153.
2. www.nytimes.com/1979/03/12/archives/segovia-gives-recital-at-the-white-house-us-debut-in-1928-son-in.html.
3. Segovia Obituary https://www.latimes.com/archives/la-xpm-1987-06-03-mn-2777-story.html.

Chapter 10: The Spoleto Years

1. Levett, Christian, an art collector who established a classical museum in Mougins, France and then moved to a palazzo in Florence with an extensive collection of American women artists. https://en.wikipedia.org/wiki/Mougins_Museum_of_Classical_Art; https://www.wsj.com/articles/american-women-in-florence-11611341719.
2. https://www.festivaldispoleto.com/en/spettacoli/presentazione/.

Chapter 11: Cross-cultural Challenges: *Swan Lake* to *A Chorus Line*

1. Zeffirelli, Franco. Zeffirelli sold his Villa TreVilla in 2007. It is now a luxurious hotel https://www.villatreville.com/villa-treville#tab=heritage.
2. Segal, Lewis. "Artistic Vandalism: Zeffrelli's *Swan Lake* by La Scala Ballet," *Los Angeles Times*, July 18, 1986.
3. Franko, Mark. *Martha Graham in Love and War*, Oxford University Press, New York. 2012, 17.

Chapter 12: The Mafia Reigns

1. *West Side Story* Touring. There were other productions such as the 1958 production in Manchester, England, but this was the first

Broadway production to tour Europe. https://en.wikipedia.org/wiki/West_Side_Story.

2. Mafia still has a stronghold in Italy, more so in Sicily despite attempts to contain their power. Even today, more than 25 years later, they are still a noteworthy corrupt and terrifying element in Italy. https://www.theguardian.com/world/2021/jan/13/italy-mafia-trial-ndragheta-calabria.

Chapter 14: *Tamara*

1. D'Annunzio, Gabriele. Although not known to most Americans, he is idealized in Italy as both a poet, writer, and political icon despite his fascist leanings. Every Italian school studies his poetry. https://www.britannica.com/art/autobiography-literature.
2. Blumenthal, Eileen. www.nytimes,com/1987/11/29/theatr/tamara-from-the-grouond-floor-up.html?pagewanted=all.
3. Gussow, Mel. https://timesmachine.nytimes.com/timesmachine/1987/12/03/573587.html?pageNumber=88

Chapter 15: Porgy and Me

1. The 2019 production at the Met Opera staged by Michael Yeargan has a set very similar to mine. One wonders if my set staged by Will Roberson was an inspiration?
2. Godovsky, Leopold. Stephen Sondheim, *New York Times*, Artbeat, blogs, nytimes.com 08/10/2011. He takes issue with a Broadway version that bows to the "musical" audience, compromising its operatic quality and revised characters. Leopold was extremely upset that the Gershwin heirs had bowed to monetary concerns. He passed away a few days before opening night.
3. Milnes, Rodney. Opera/*Porgy and Bess*, Festival Hall, *London Times* 9/16/1999. Underscored the high quality of the production.
4. Baker, Josephine; performed at Folies Bergère. Josephine Baker: *L'etoile noire des Folies Bergère*, 1926–1932.

5. Interesting to note that despite racism in federal and state policies, *Porgy and Bess* was selected in 1952 as an American opera for touring by the State Department. https://en.wikipedia.org/wiki/Porgy_and_Bess.

Chapter 16: Black and White

1. https://www.rodrodgersdance.org/rod-rodgers).
2. Baldwin, James. "On Catfish Row" Review originally published in *Commentary*, September 1959.
3. Noonan, Ellen. *The Strange Career of Porgy and Bess*. Race, Culture, and America's Most Famous Opera. University of North Carolina Press, 2012. Striking that the extensive analysis of the opera in *The Strange Career of Porgy & Bess* makes no mention of the detective.
4. Pollack, Howard, *George Gershwin, His Life and Work*, 607.
5. *Broadway World*, August 26, 2019 "Over 3 decades of performances MAMA, I WANT TO SING Celebrates Anniversary with Return to Original Theater".
6. Hersch, Charles, *Jews and Jazz*, Copyright 2017 Routledge, 31 by BWW News Desk Aug. 26, 2019.
7. Shadle, Douglas W. "Confronting a Complex Legacy," *New York Times*, Sunday, March 21, 2021, Art and Leisure, 11.

Bibliography

Christiansen, Rupert. *Diaghilev's Empire: How the Ballet Russes Enthralled the World*. Farrar, Straus and Giroux. 2022.

Claridge, Laura. *Tamara de Lempicka: A Life of Deco and Decadence*. New York: Clarkson Potter. 1999.

Cohen, Roger. *The Girl from Human Street: A Jewish Family Odyssey*. New York: Knopf Doubleday Publishing Group. 2015.

De Mille, Agnes. *Where the Wings Grow: A Memoir of Childhood*. New York: Doubleday Books. 1978.

Drummond, John. *Speaking of Diaghilev*. London: Faber & Faber, Inc. 1997.

Duarte, John W. *Andrés Segovia, As I Knew Him*. St. Louis: Mel Bay Publications, Inc. 1998.

Foulkes, Julia L. *Modern Bodies: Dance and American Modernism from Martha Graham to Alvin Ailey*. Chapel Hill: The University of North Carolina Press. 2002.

Foulkes, Julia L. *A Place for Us: "West Side Story" and New York*. Chicago: University of Chicago Press. 2016.

Franko, Mark. *Martha Graham in Love and War: The Life in the Work.* New York: Oxford University Press. 2012.

Harris, Andrea. *Making Ballet American: Modernism Before and Beyond Balanchine.* New York: Oxford University Press. 2017.

Homans, Jennifer. *Apollo's Angels: A History of Ballet.* New York: Random House Trade Paperbacks. 2011.

Ioanid, Radu. *The Holocaust in Romania: The Destruction of Jews and Gypsies Under the Antonescu Regime, 1940–1944.* Chicago: Ivan R. Dee, Inc. 2008.

Ioanid, Radu. *The Ransom of the Jews: The Story of the Extraordinary Secret Bargain Between Romania and Israel.* Chicago: Ivan R. Dee, Inc. 2005.

Levy, Reynold. *They Told Me Not To Take the Job.* PublicAffairs Edition. 2015.

Noonan, Ellen. *The Strange Career of Porgy and Bess: Race, Culture, and America's Most Famous Opera.* Chapel Hill: The University of North Carolina Press. 2014.

Pollack, Howard. *George Gershwin: His Life and Work.* Oakland: University of California Press. 2007.

Robinson, Harlow. *The Last Impresario: The Life, Times and Legacy of Sol Hurok.* New York: Viking Press. 1994.

Segovia, Andrés. *Segovia: An Autobiography of the Years 1893–1920.* New York: Macmillan Publishing Co. 1976.

Wallach, Amei. *Taking Venice: The Rauschenberg Factor.* Directed/ Written by Amei Wallach. Trailer. Film not released.

Index

A

A Chorus Line tour
　Nervi festival, 123–125
　Puccini Festival, 119, 125–126
　reviews, 125
Aborn, Louis, 153
Adams, Aubrey, 74
AEA (Actors' Equity Association),
　West Side Story extension
　request, 132–133
Ailey, Alvin, 164
Ain't Misbehavin', 164, 168
Algaroff, Youly, 121
Ambakaila, 68–69, 74–75
　cultural issues, 167
　management from hospital, 80
Andreano, Michele, 134
Antonescu, Ion, 2
Arpino, Gerald, 136
Asami, Maki, 112–113
Asami Maki Ballet, 112

ATER, 68–70
Augustine, Rose, 83–84
Australia tour of *Porgy and Bess*, 177

B

Badini, Carlo, 113–114
Badini, Maria, 94
Balanchine, George, 69–70, 88–89
Ballets de Monte Carlo, 127–128
Ballets de Monte Carlo tour,
　Robert, Dornhelm, 128–129
Ballets Russes de Monte Carlo, 128
Ballets Trocadero de Monte Carlo, 99
Barnes, Clive, 65–66
Barnett, Robert, 99
Baryshnikov, Mikhail, 88–89, 114
Beijing tour of *Porgy and Bess*
　(The People's Great Hall),
　185–187
Benhur, Oded, 142
Santi, Franco Biondi, 143–144

Bett, Patricia Murray, 193
Bisset, Jacqueline, 122
Blache-Gill, Gail, 174
Black Americans
　discrimination on *Porgy and Bess* tour, 170
　early rejection of *Porgy and Bess*, 173
Black artists
　Gershwin's affinity for Black-American music, 174
　Harlem Gospel Choir, 172
　Marie Brooks Pan African Dance Company, 170–171
　The New York Express, 171
　promoting, 168–169
Blaska, Felix, 99
Borsellino, Paolo, 136
Break Dancers, 171
Brooks, Marie, 170
Bruhn, Erik, 60
Bubbling Brown Sugar, 164
Bucharest, trip with George Reisner, 23–24
Buenos Aires, Teatro Colon, 153
Buona Fortuna!, 133–134
Butoh, Japanese dance movement, 102
Byakko Sha, 102–103
　Ohsuka, Isamu, 102–103

Cairo tour of *Porgy and Bess*, 178–184
cargo plane to St. Louis, 120
Caribbean trip, 47
Caroline (Princess of Monaco), 127–128
Castello Sforzesco, 112
Cavalli, Lietta, 140
Celeste, 193
Centinari, Letizia, 112
Central Park Sheraton job, 44
Cheetham, Deborah, 177
Chicken Shit Hill, 101
Children of Theater Street, 61, 128
Christmas, Milan, 37
cin cin, 112–113
civil rights movement, 166
Clarke, Martha, 99
Cohen, Moti, 64
Cohen, Shosh, 64
Cohen, Steve, 160
Crowsnest, 99
cultural issues. *See also* race issues
　Ambakaila, 167
　Asami Make Ballet troupe, 112–113
　Italians and American culture, 94
　nuances of performances, audience and, 126
　Trinidad and Tobago trip, 167
Cunningham, Merce, 69

C
Caceres, Richard, 132
Cahalan, Joseph, 168
Caio Melisso, 99

D
Dance Theater of Harlem, 164
D'Annunzio, Gabriele, 146
de la Rocha, Alicia, 84

Index

de Lempicka, Kizette, 148
de Lempicka, Tamara, 146
de Mille, Agnes, 84
  Where the Wings Grow, 129
Dias, Paulo, 172
Dobosh Torte, 4
Dornhelm, Bandi, 27
Dornhelm, Edith, 27
  visit, 41–42
Dornhelm, Robert
  Ballets de Monte Carlo tour, 128–129
  Children of Theater Street, 61, 128
Douglas, Scott, 98, 101
Dreyfus on Devil's Island, opening night problems, 65–66

E

Eloise (Thompson), 141
  Klein, Nadia, and, 142
emigration, family's petitions, 10

F

Fame, 133
Farber, John, 44
Farber, Maia, 44
Fatima (au pair) visa issues, 103–106
Feld Ballet, 89
Ferrara, Giorgio, 109–110
Festival delle Ville Vesuviane, 107–108
Festival of Two Worlds, 109
Finch, Stephen, 162
fireworks show TT 60, 156–157
Fracci, Carla, 118–119

G

Gemes, Juno, 177
Gershwin, Arthur, 157
Gershwin, George, 142–143
  Black-American music and, 174
Gershwin, Marc, 157
Godowsky, Elaine, 161
Godowsky, Frances, 143
Godowsky, Leopold, 142–143, 157, 158, 161
Godunov, Alexander, 120–122
  Caracas with Jacqueline Bisset, 122
Godunov in Caracas, 122
Godunov in Rome, 121–122
Gody, Carrie "Schatzi," 44
Gold, Shelley, 67
Göröcs, Zoltán, 67–68
Graham, Martha, 129
  Where the Wings Grow (de Mille), 129
Graham Company, 129
grandparents, 3
Green Card acquisition, 45, 49
Groder, Mike, 75–77

H

Harlem Gospel Choir, 172
Harlem Swing, 168
Havas, Agnes, 168
Hawkins, Eric, 129–130
Heifetz, Daniel, 56
Higginsen, Vy, 172
Hoyt, Jennifer, 162

Hurok, Sol
  bomb, 58
  death, 65
  Metropolitan Opera, 60–61
  Nureyev, Rudolph, 59–60
  Prude, Walter, 54
  Segovia tour manager, 54
  Semenoff, Simon and, 52–53

I
INS interaction, 47–49
International Concert Management (ICM), 68
Israel, 29–33
Italy
  Florence, 36
  Italians and American culture, 94
  Milan, 36–38
    Christmas, 37
  traditionalism, 95

J
Japan, ohnsen visit, 150–151
Jewish Agency for Israel, shacks for immigrants, 29
Jewish communities in Transylvania, 1
Jewish Defense League, bomb in Sol Hurok office, 58
Joffrey, Robert, 136
Joffrey Ballet, 85
Joseph, Cuthbert, 74–75
Joyce, Van, 96
Judaism, religions practices in Timişoara, 17–18

K
The Kaye Playhouse, 65
KGB, kidnap of grandmother, 14–15
Kibbutz Kfar Blum, 29–30
Klein, Andrew, 4–13
Klein, Eugene (grandfather), 3
Klein, Gabriel (brother)
  birth, 7
  Lohamei HaGetaot, 30
Klein, George, 4
Klein, Nadia
  birth, 90
  Eloise and, 142
Kleyman, Marta "Maki," 44
Kone, Iris, 58
Krausz, Adrienne and Leslie, 43
Krizanc, John, 146
Kurtzer, Daniel C., 178
  Sesame Street production, 184

L
La Scala, 94
  Badini, Carlo, 113–114
  Castello Sforzesco performances, 112
  Centinari, Letizia, 112
  first time seeing, 38
  il Sovrintendente, 112
  influence long term, 111–112
  National Ballet of Canada, 127
La Scala Ballet
  cargo plane to St. Louis, 120
  Fracci, Carla, 118–119

Index

MUNI and, 115–117
  tour, 115–116
  tour offer, 114–115
Lang, Jacques, 69
Lang, Pearl, 129
Levrero, Alessandro, *A Chorus Line Tour* issues, 123–125
Li Lanqing, 186–187
Living Arts, Inc., 90–91
  inception, 65
  as rebirth, 94–95
  visitor tours of New York, 96
Loporto, Marisa, 152
Lorimer, Michael, 56

M

Maazel, Lorin, 114–115
Mafia
  Borsellino, Paolo, car bomb, 136
  Falcone, Giovanni, assassination, 136
  protection fees, 136
Makarova, Natalia, 85
Marie Brooks Pan African Dance Company, 170–171
Martelli, Maria Paola, 140
"Masters Festival for the Performance Arts," 67
Mavodin, Ica, 39
McBride, Patricia, 88–89
McClellan, Casey, 135
Menotti, Francis "Chip," 109
Menotti, Gian Carlo, 94
  Festival of Two Worlds, 109
Meyer, Kitty, 45–46

  death, 151–152
Metropolitan Opera, Hurok, Sol, 60–61
Milstein, Nathan, 67
Minnelli, Liza
  Gershwin, George, 142–143
  meeting Oded Benhur, 142
  Nice meeting, 139–140
  physical limitations, performance and, 141
  Thompson, Kay, 141
Mouchtar-Samorai, David, 64
  opening night problems, 65–66
Mukamal, Steve, 48–49

N

Naci (grandmother), 3
  KGB kidnapping, 14–15
  music influences, 39–40
  trauma of leaving Romania, 27
Naim, Jojo, 75
National Ballet of Canada, 127
Nazis
  Final Solution, 2
  Hungary alliance, 2
  Romania alliance, 2
neck injury in car accident, 77–80
New York, 43–45
New Zealand tour of *Porgy and Bess*, 177
Nureyev, Rudolf
  final performance at Festival delle Ville Vesuviane, 107–108
  massage, 59–60
  Nuereyev and Friends tours, 60

O

Ohsuka, Isamu, 102–103
Ottolenghi, Vittoria, 99, 108

P

Palermo
  Arpino, Gerald, 136
  The Joffrey Ballet, 135, 137
  Opera dei Pupi, 135–136
  Parco della Favorita, 135–136
Parson Weems and the Cherry Tree, 129–130
Peace Treaty of Passarowitz, 1
Piovesan, Silvano, 68
Piroska, Szilàgyi (grandmother). See Naci (grandmother)
Porgy and Bess as quintessential, 153
  92nd Street Y, 161
  Australia and New Zealand tour, 177
  Beijing tour, 185–187
  Black members, 160
  Cairo tour, 178–184
  Charleston opening, 159
  Cohen, Steve, 160
  discrimination on American tour, 170
  early Black theatregoers' reactions, 173
  Finch, Stephen, 162
  Gershwin heirs, 153
  Gershwin's Jewish roots, 174
  Graham, Elizabeth, 164
  Hoyt, Jennifer, 162
  Israel tour, 189–191
  non-Black composer, issues, 167–168
  as quintessential American opera, 173
  Roberson, Will, 158–159
  Russia tour, 187–188
  Takada, Tokichi, 154–155
  Teatro Colon opening night, 156
  touring production, licensing, 158
  white character, 168
  Williams, Susan, 162–164
  productions by year, 197–207
Prude, Walter, 54, 67

R

race issues. *See also* cultural issues; Black Americans; Black artists
  civil rights movement, 166
  discrimination on *Porgy and Bess* tour, 170
  paradoxes in the arts, 169–171
  Porgy and Bess non-Black composer, 167–168
  promoting Black artists, 168–169
RAI Italian TV, 116
Ransohoff, Joseph, 79
Ransohoff, Rita, 79
Rauschenberg, Robert, 69
Ray, Gene Anthony, 133–134
"Red Wheelbarrow" (Williams), 71–72
red wheelbarrows of life, 78, 168
Reisner, George, 23
Ristorante Baronessa, 140

Index

River Café, 96
Robbins, Jerome, 131–132
Roberson, Will, 158–159, 162
Robert Desrosiers Dance Company of Canada, 107
Robins, Gene, 66–67
Rod Rodgers Dance Company, 67
Romania
  Antonescu, Ion, 2
  Bessarabia massacre, 2
  Communist takeover, 7–8
  leaving, 25–26
  Nazi alliance, 2
  North Bukovina massacre, 2
  Transylvania, Timișoara, 1
Rondo, George, 147
Roseman, Ralph, 131
Rounseville, Ellen, 43–44
Russia tour of *Porgy and Bess*, 187–188

S

Santi, Franco Biondi, 143–144
Segovia, Andrés, 54
  anti-Semitism, 86
  class structure opinions, 57–58
  death, 91
  end of relationship, 90–91
  first assignment, 54–55
  forgotten guitar, 90
  and Nadia Klein, 90
  post-concert dinners with, 56–57
  provincialism, 84–85
  and Rose Augustine, 83–84
  visit after neck injury, 80
  White House concert, 86–88
Segovia, Carlos, 86–87
Segovia, Emilita, 86–87
Semenoff, Simon, first meeting, 52
Simonini, Marilla, 137
Simring, Steve, 168
Soresi, Giovanni, 145
Spoleto, 93–100
  Ballets Trocadero de Monte Carlo, 99
  Byakko Sha, 102–103
  Count Datti, 101–102
  Crowsnest, 99
  Ferrara, Giorgio, 109–110
  Festival of Two Worlds, 109
  Il Mulino visit, 97–98
  Il Re della Danza, 97
  Phyllis' encounter with motorcyclists, 109
  return in 1983, 100–101
SS Stella Solaris, 35
Stahl, David, 161
Sterzi, Adriana, dinner invitation, 145–146
Strunsky, Mike, 157
Swan Lake tour, 114–115
  Fracci, Carla, 118–119
  open-air performance issues, 116–117
  plane cargo to St. Louis, 120
Szeryng, Henryk, 67

T

Takada, Tokichi, 154–155
  birthday fireworks, 156–157

Tamara, 145–152
 audience dress, 148
 casting, 147
 de Lempicka, Kizette, 148
 Japan shows, 149–150
 Krizanc, John, 146
 press conference in Italian, 147
 Villa Brasini, 147
 Villa Erba, 147
taxi skiing, 22
Tchernichova, Elena, 121–122
Teatro Colon, 153
 Porgy and Bess opening night, 156
Testa, Alberto, 99, 108
Tetley, Glen, 98, 101
The Joffrey Ballet, 135, 137
The New York Express, 171
The October Bridge (Egypt), 182–183
The Rod Rodgers Dance Company, 166
Théâtre du Châtelet, *West Side Story*, 69
Thompson, Kay, 141
Timişoara, 1
 early life
 bicycling, 11–12
 grandmother's kidnapping, 14–15
 languages, 19–20
 religious practices, 17–18
 sports, 21
 tennis, 12–13
 yearly pig purchase, 16–17
 Great Synagogue (Sinagoga Cetate), 17–18

 pre-1948, 8
 taxi skiing, 22
 Timişoara University of Agriculture, 21
Transylvania
 Jewish communities, 1
 Timişoara, 1
Trinidad and Tobago trip, 74–76
 Minister of Culture, 167
 Perle Mesta, 167
Troy, Doris, 172

U

Union. See AEA (Actors' Equity Association)
Urman, Phyllis
 courtship, 72–73
 meeting, 72

V

Vágó Margaret, 19
Ventura, Diana Geffner, 159
Vienna, return to, 41–42

W

Watts, Heather, 88–89
Weizman, Ezer, 189
West Side Story
 Palermo, 137
 Théâtre du Châtelet, 69
 touring, 131–132
Where the Wings Grow (de Mille), 84, 129
Wiener, Ari (mother), 4
 depression, 13–14

Index

dobosh torte, 4
half-brother, 15–16
marriage to Andrew, 5
Wiener, Gyuri (Uncle), 23
Wiener, Vera (Aunt), 23
Wilcox, Charlotte, 131
Williams, Susan, 162
Williams, William Carlos, 71–72
Wilson, John, 59
Wohlstein, Leopold, 3
Wydro, Ken, 172

Z
Zeffirelli, Franco, 114–117

About the Authors

*P*hyllis Urman-Klein, PhD, is both a psychoanalyst and couple/family therapist who had adjunct faculty appointments at Cornell and Mt. Sinai Medical Schools. In addition to her professional career, she has been a Patron of the Season in the Gardens of La Pietra in Florence, Italy, as well as a member of the International Council at the Grey Gallery from 2004-2010. She currently maintains a private practice in New York City.

*P*eter Klein has been active in the performing arts for more than 40 years. He was among the first to export American dance, orchestrating American Ballet Theatre's first Italian engagement and working with icons ranging from Andrès Segovia to Martha Graham. He was also a pioneer in introducing American musicals to international audiences, serving as the force behind the first-ever non-State Department-run touring productions such as *West Side Story* and *A Chorus Line*. His groundbreaking production of George Gershwin's *Porgy and Bess* has been touring the globe since 1992. He resides in New York City and Toscana with his wife. www.peterkleinyc.com

www.ingramcontent.com/pod-product-compliance
Lightning Source LLC
Chambersburg PA
CBHW020656060526
44119CB00090B/407/J